My Sister Bootsy

A Portrait of Trudy Silverheels

Miranda Whitecrow

ARCHER TRENT, PUBLISHER
2018

This is a work for hire, commissioned by the Griffoun Society, of which the author Miranda Whitecrow is a member.

Front Cover Art: *A Portrait of Trudy Silverheels*
Copyright © 2009 Ihar Balailkin

2nd Edition
Februarry 6, 2019
Archer Trent, Publisher
Houston Texas

ISBN 978-0-9990029-8-8

Miranda (Dusty) Whitecrow
Née Blanca Miranda Cuervo
July 20, 1982, near Bagdad, Arizona

Trudy Lynn (Bootsy) Silverheels
Née Linda Yazzie
June 13, 1986, near Bagdad, Arizona

A NOTE FROM THE AUTHOR

Two of the books Bootsy has written (*The Chosen Profession of Jade Stonecalf* and *Nuevo Biloxi*) are pure fiction. The other two (*Baring All* and *Dusky Nightshade and the Little Heathens*) are true, except that some of the names have been changed to conceal the real identities of certain individuals. In this current volume, I have followed Bootsy's lead and employed the same false names to identify those particular individuals that she felt needed to be protected. Otherwise, this is as honest an account as my memory is capable of providing.

For our mother:
Judith Begay

SELF-PORTRAIT
FROM THE SKETCHBOOK OF
TRUDY LYNN (BOOTSY) SILVERHEELS

I
BURIED ALIVE

My sister Bootsy—whom you may know as *Trudy Silverheels*—nearly died last year. She and I were taking pictures in the back garden of her little retreat house behind my home in Mexico City when the ground beneath our feet collapsed. I tumbled perhaps ten or twelve feet into a great hole that opened up. I broke my arm in the process, but I was able to scramble out and go for help. Bootsy, however, was plunged much deeper into the abyss, and then as debris followed her down, she was buried alive. For me the ordeal was a nightmare experience, but Bootsy does not even remember it.

1

She had, the day before, flown down from Houston, and her last memory from before the accident was of being on the airplane. She has told me that it was her initial assumption upon returning to full consciousness weeks later that the plane had crashed.

When emergency workers dug down to her, they found her unconscious and barely clinging to life. Yet her arms were wrapped protectively around her belly. Eight months pregnant and comatose, she was not initially given very good odds of recovering. The doctors at the ABC (American British Cowdray Hospital) insisted that any slim chance of survival she might have depended upon her being delivered immediately by cesarean section of the twins she carried. This might also be the babies' best chance, they told us.

Names had but recently been settled upon. First into the world was Mindy Alexandra, whose birth weight was recorded at four pounds, seven ounces. Paige Veronica, two ounces heavier, was delivered moments later. They appeared to be perfectly identical, healthy, and uninjured by the accident that still threatened their mother's life.

When, four days after the accident, I finally got around to telephoning Bootsy's girlfriend Parivash Jamshidi in Houston to let her know what had happened, she immediately assumed that Bootsy's mishap had resulted from the earthquake that had just struck southern Mexico. I set her straight and apologized for not having called sooner. She was very understanding and even offered to help me notify Bootsy's other friends, especially those whose email addresses could be found in Bootsy's art studio in Houston. As it turned out, she was able to do even better than that; she found my sister's password and opened her Yahoo account to tell everyone who tried to initiate a chat there.

The earthquake brought a lot of destruction to many parts of Mexico City, but our neighborhood, San Ángel, and nearby Coyoacán, were mostly spared. Certainly our two houses, which back up to each other, suffered no damage. The newspapers were full of rescue operations and reports of the death toll. Our back–yard cave-in, which had initially attracted so much media attention, was immediately forgotten.

For weeks Bootsy remained in a coma. Yet for some reason the doctors now seemed somewhat more optimistic regarding her likelihood of survival. Mother and I took turns sitting by her bed, holding her hand, talking to her. Once, during the second week, I saw her smile just faintly and her fingers twitch. From that instant, I knew that she was on her way back to us. The lights were still out, but in the darkness she was healing herself.

Then one day, without fanfare, she was awake and looking about, rather like a person seeing the world for the first time. She did not speak or even attempt to communicate. If someone asked her a question or tried to engage her in conversation, she just smiled beatifically, but answered not. The doctors feared that she might be aphasic. But if that were the case, one would have expected her to be in a panic about it. I believe she simply had nothing to say. She was marshaling all her energies toward her recovery.

Given a pad of paper and a pencil, she made no effort to write, but drew pictures instead, yet nothing germane to questions being put to her. We were not even sure that she recognized any of us. The smile she blessed me and other family members with was no different than the one she bestowed upon nurses and orderlies. Because of her sweet nature, Bootsy quickly became a hospital favorite. Everyone loved her.

When her catheter was removed, she was able to use a bed pan, but she would never request it. She would merely wait patiently for someone to bring it and hold it in place. Asked whether she would prefer to use the toilet, she remained unresponsive. So I took it on myself to help her out of bed and lead her by the arm to the bathroom. There she knew exactly what to do and required no help.

But she was alarmed by her own reflection in the mirror. Her head had been partly shaved in order for her skull to be trepanned; so the hair on one side remained long while the other side exhibited only stubble. A slight frown came on her face as she stared into the glass. Back in bed she drew pictures of herself (amazingly accurate likenesses) with long flowing hair, such as she had worn in high school. Her hair had not been that long in seven or eight years. A tear rolled down her cheek.

The next morning she was again at work executing self-portraits, except now all her sketches showed her with a totally bald head. This was a real attempt at communication. I understood exactly what she wanted. I called in a beautician, who carefully shaved Bootsy's head. Her hair would grow back, but it would all be the same length as it did so.

Get-well wishes poured in from all over the United States, as well as from Canada, India, Russia, the Philippines, Japan, Uganda, Belarus, France, England, Ireland, Argentina, Colombia, and

Morocco. I was amazed at how many friends my little sister had around the globe. True, she was something of a minor celebrity, being the author of two books. However, neither of those books could yet be called a huge success. Was it possible that these well-wishers were all fans of hers (readers of her books)? Or were they close personal friends? From the tone of most of the letters, I should probably guess the latter. I kept up with every single one; for I knew that someday Bootsy would wish to respond.

It was evident that she had suffered brain injury. What was not yet known was the degree to which she might hope to recover.   Her doctors recommended that she soon be transferred to Memorial Hermann Hospital in Houston. This was where Congresswoman Giffords, the previous year, had been sent for therapy following her initial recovery from the assassination attempt in Arizona. Happily, my husband Geoffrey and I were in a financial position to make this happen.

But Mother and Gran both needed to be convinced that this was indeed the best course of action. For days we argued the matter, exploring other options as well, and sometimes the debate became quite heated. Nor were we always careful to take our discussion out of Bootsy's presence.

Finally, one evening Bootsy surprised us all by interrupting the goings-on, uttering her first word since the accident: "Houston."

My sister has, for several years, made her primary home in Houston. So it was natural that she would wish to return there. But did she mean to do therapy at Memorial Hermann? I asked her if that were her intention.

"Tomorrow," she answered.

"Sweetie, I don't think we can arrange it that quickly."

"Tomorrow," she repeated firmly.

Getting Bootsy checked out of the hospital the very next day was an undertaking, but we managed it and took her to Mother's apartment house in Coyoacán to spend the night. My husband Geoffrey chartered a private jet to fly her and our cousin Michelle Nakai, who had been elected her caretaker, to Houston the following day. Michelle was living then at Crownpoint, New Mexico, but insomuch as she considered herself Bootsy's "blood brother," she had immediately, upon hearing of the accident, flown to Mexico City to keep vigil with Mother and me by Bootsy's bedside.

Tonight Bootsy would have a chance to see her babies for the first time. She touched their cheeks tentatively, then held them in her arms, one at a time. She gazed very tenderly at them, I thought. But she remained taciturn. So it was difficult to tell exactly how she was feeling and whether or not she was connecting with them at any but a superficial level. I wondered if she would ever be a real mother to them. They might well be walking and talking by the time she were able to assume responsibility for their day-to-day care.

With two daughters of my own, I was prepared to take these two dear babies into my own home and keep them indefinitely. I had the help of reliable and devoted household servants; so I should not even feel stressed. But for my sister's sake, I hated to think that she might miss out on any of the joys of motherhood.

"Is Aunt Bootsy going to stay retarded forever?" Morgan, my seven-year-old, wanted to know.

I was horrified that she would say such a thing in front of her aunt, but before I could chastise her, Bootsy, without saying a word, silenced and then reassured me. My sister and I have always been able to communicate effectively with just a glance. Given only the tiniest clue, we can read each other's mind.

Immediately after the accident, Geoffrey and the girls and I had moved out of our own house. We had feared that the cave-in might spread outward, for we had initially assumed the cause to be eroding limestone, and until we knew the extent of it, we would be living in a hotel. I prayed we would not lose our home forever, but I was not very hopeful. As it turned out, however, the cavern beneath our property was an ancient excavation shored up with massive timbers, which had finally rotted away. The apparent purpose of this underground vault was to conceal an armory. A date carved on one of the broken beams read either AD 1536 or possibly AD 1586. The chamber was found to be filled with what would have been invaluable treasures had not rot and rust already had their way so totally. The army was called in to take away twenty-one barrels of black powder. The remainder of the stash got buried under tons and tons of concrete. Nothing was deemed salvageable, but our home and Bootsy's little house were both saved.

Within days of her return to Houston, Bootsy was speaking in whole (albeit simple) sentences. Occasionally she did have difficulty remembering particular words. This caused her great conster-nation. And yet the rest of us were very encouraged by the progress she was making. However, as her communication skills improved, other memory issues began to be apparent. She had no difficulty recalling names, faces, or incidents from before the accident. But an important conversation she had had just the day before might be totally forgotten. Bootsy spent only ten days in hospital in Houston before being released to continue her therapy as an outpatient.

Because Geoffrey's work so often takes him to Houston, we own a house there as well. Actually, it is in Clear Lake, which is rather on the outskirts of the city. Clear Lake is where NASA is, by the way. This house was where Bootsy would be staying with our cousin Michelle as her companion. Already in residence there was Bootsy's friend Carlita Wakiya, an Apache girl, whom Bootsy herself had persuaded me the previous year to employ as our house-sitter. We usually spent only a few weeks a year in Houston; so it was important to have someone living in our house whilst we were away. Bootsy herself had once performed this service for us, but when she had wanted to start spending more time in her art studio near downtown Houston, she had recommended Carlita as her replacement.

Every day now Michelle drove Bootsy into town to spend hours in therapy. Because my sister was consistently cheerful and never made the least complaint, she quickly became a favorite with staff at Memorial Hermann, as she had been at the ABC. Then after a nurse's aide recognized her from the photo on the back of one of her books and asked for an autograph, she began to be treated like a celebrity. Almost every day thereafter she was asked to sign books. Nothing in the world could have pleased her more. She told me once that she liked signing books almost as much as she likes sex, and that, if you know my sister, is saying quite a lot.

Incidentally, Bootsy's handwriting changed significantly as a result of her head trauma. She had to make a real effort in order to make her new signature resemble, in more than a superficial way, her old signature. And it is still not a very good match. Barclay's Bank was not easily persuaded that she was indeed herself.

More and more frequently now, Bootsy would give Michelle the slip in order to visit her numerous "sex friends" (both male and female) in the Houston area. She had missed them, of course, and likewise the pleasures she had previously been wont to share with them. She now seemed intent upon making up for lost time. Many an evening she failed to return to the house in Clear Lake, staying out all night and causing Michelle great anxiety for her well-being.

In August, Mother took a frantic call from Michelle, who was at her wits' end. She wanted guidance. What should she do? But Mother, mindful of how strong-willed Bootsy had always been, didn't have an immediate answer. Mother called me for advice, and I called Gran in Arizona. Gran immediately caught a plane to Houston and laid down the law. Gran is the only person whose word Bootsy will always heed.

In any event, Bootsy did, indeed, start taking better care of herself, or rather she started allowing Michelle to do her job of looking after her. And Bootsy greatly surprised her therapy team by the rapidity of her improvement. They had initially told her that she might have to continue with that regimen for as long as two years, but after only a few months, she was demanding to be cut lose. And no one could cite any valid reason to keep her in therapy.

The accident had occurred on March 18, 2012. By autumn of that year Bootsy was ready to return to Mexico City to assume her mommy role. It had originally been her plan to give birth in Mexico City, where she would have the help and support of both Mother and me whilst the babies were little. Then as they got older, she had meant to take them to our grandmother's ranch in Arizona, where we ourselves (Bootsy and I) had enjoyed an idyllic childhood. There Michelle would join her to share parenting responsibilities with her.

Bootsy, you see, had no intention of legally marrying or living with the babies' father, but she was wise enough to realize that she would need help. Michelle, also single and very fond of children, was the ideal candidate. She has been Bootsy's closest friend and confidant since childhood.

But now the plan was changed. The twins were by this time so much a part of my household that Bootsy could not bear to tear them away. She even allowed them to stay in their same nursery when, at night, she went to bed in her own little house in back. She spent more than two months in Mexico City before announcing that she was returning to Houston to pick up her art career. She was convinced, she said, that the best interest of Mindy and Paige would be served by her leaving them here in my care. I agreed.

Bootsy had not participated in her babies' birth; she had not nursed them as she had wanted to; and she did not know them as I did. At a glance, I could tell which was which; she could not distinguish them apart (and still cannot).

Oh, she loves them and would do anything for them, even sacrifice her very life if necessary. But somehow she has not the same spiritual connection to them that I quickly developed. I bless her for being so unselfish as to allow their lives not to be disrupted by an unnecessary change that could only have served to boost her ego.

I, for my part, promised her that I would never come between her and them, never limit her visits, never sue for custody, never attempt to deny her the right to take them away should she choose to do so, even years from now. I asked my own daughters Madeleine and Morgan to refrain from calling me *Mommy* in front of the twins, because I want them to have no difficulty identifying my sister as their mother.

In short, Bootsy and I are both doing everything we can to make this work to the benefit of all concerned.

The only loser, I fear, could be Michelle, who has already sold her house in Crownpoint, and now has nowhere to live. Geoffrey and I offered her a place

17

in our home here in Mexico City, but she declined. Gran hopes, I believe, that Michelle will elect to move to the ranch as originally planned. Gran could certainly use her help with that operation, and Michelle could hope to inherit someday. Gran is painfully aware that none of her obvious heirs are even remotely interested in taking over the ranch. I love the place, but my life is in Mexico City. The same can be said of Mother. And only to bring the twins up there would Bootsy have moved to such a remote location. She has to be where she can attend art shows and salons, where she can easily get to book signings and TV interviews. In any event, I hope Michelle accepts Gran's invitation. I think she will. ❧

II
OUR CHILDHOOD IN ARIZONA

I was a month shy of my fourth birthday when Bootsy was born. Perhaps by oversight, I was allowed to be present at her birth. The baby was coming fast, and nobody made the effort to shoo me out of the room; so I parked myself out of the way in an overstuffed arm chair in the farthest corner and tried to be inconspicuous. Mother passed out —fainted, I suppose—just as my new little sister entered the world. The panic in the room intensified. Gran quickly wrapped the newborn in a bath towel and laid her in my lap to hold whilst she herself attended our mother. There was a doctor present, but not an MD. He was an elderly veterinarian, who, if I recall correctly, had been called to the ranch to tend to a sick horse. I suppose it must have been a big surprise for him to have to deliver a human baby.

In the movies, births are always announced by loud wails. But Bootsy did not cry; she just looked around with seemingly keen interest at this strange place that was to be her new home. When she gazed up into my eyes, my heart melted. In that moment a bond stronger than steel was formed between us, and we have remained close ever since. Not once in twenty-seven years have we bickered or quarreled. We don't always see eye to eye about everything, but the affection and respect we feel for each other is so great that disagreements never lead to bad feelings or harsh words.

When the doctors were telling us, after the cave-in a year ago last spring, that the prognosis for Bootsy's survival was very poor, I simply could not get my mind around the possibility of a world in which she did not exist. Television presenters are always going on about "larger-than-life" personalities, but the only individual I have ever encountered who could accurately be described that way is my sister Bootsy.

When I was seven and she was three, I taught her how to read. A few years later I taught her how to French-kiss. I think that may be the last thing of any great importance that I was ever able to teach her, for by the time she started school, she had become the master; and I, her devoted disciple. Oh, I still possessed more acquired knowledge, but she had the greater wisdom, and I knew it. I was more than glad to allow her to assume the leadership rôle in our relationship. I should happily have followed her anywhere.

I have no idea whether Bootsy's IQ has ever been tested, but there can be no doubt that she is a certifiable genius. Her mind works at lightning speed; she can figure out a solution for almost any problem in less time than it would take most people to grasp the nature of the problem. I cannot tell you how many times she has amazed me that way. Were her interest in computers and technology, she'd probably be the queen of all geeks. But it is the humanities that have always held the greatest appeal for her. She knew when she was eight years old that she was going to be a writer someday. And she has never wavered from that ambition. Eventually she became an artist and a photographer as well, but writing remains her primary occupation.

Bootsy is athletic and coordinated. She's a better-than-average equestrienne and a great dancer. She swims, hikes and climbs, enjoys camping, loves contract bridge, and plays tennis like a pro. She is not, however, good at everything. She forced herself to learn Spanish, but the truth is, she's far from fluent. She has little faculty for foreign languages, and I find that extremely odd. She's not very good either at advanced mathematics. Oh, she adored basic algebra, geometry, and trigonometry, the applications of which were immediately obvious to her, but calculus and quadratic equations she found deadly boring, because they seemed to her so pointless.

But Bootsy's strongest suit is her instinctual understanding of human nature. She can, simply by looking into people's eyes or by exchanging a few words with them, know what's in their hearts; she has always been able to do this. Recalling the character of Counselor Deanna Troi on the *Next Generation Star Trek* television series, I used to tell schoolmates my little sister was an "empath." Even Mother and Gran were known to rely on Bootsy's judgment about the integrity and intentions of their lovers, as well as those of wranglers seeking employment at the ranch and of horse-traders hoping to do business with us, and this before she was ten years old.

Maturity, I suppose, is the quality that most distinguishes my sister. She was always more grown up than her years. Even today, in her twenties, she consistently exhibits better judgment than do most people with twice her age. At four years old, she wasn't like a child at all, but more like a tiny adult. Everyone said so.

In my mind's eye, I can see her now the way she looked then, pink boots on her feet, tight-fitting jeans, western shirt, and a straw cowboy hat (also pink) with a long pheasant feather stuck in the band. It was her assigned duty to take charge of all visitors to the ranch, show them around, and answer their questions honestly. This she did with total aplomb and absolute self-confidence. She then turned them over to Gran in such a good mood that, whatever business had brought them to us, a favorable outcome was all but assured.

God, how I admired her! I wanted to be just like her. And she, in turn, wanted to be just like Gran.

"I believe I'd like to try a cup of coffee," she announced one morning at breakfast. She was barely four years old. Gran drank her coffee black with no sugar; so naturally, that's how Bootsy wanted hers.

Nobody expected her to like the black sludge; so rather than argue with her, Mother simply poured her a cup, which Bootsy downed before it had a chance to cool.

"I reckon I'll be having coffee with my breakfast every morning from now on," she informed us.

Gran and Mother were highly amused, and neither wanted to deny her. But they were concerned that caffeine might not be very healthy for one as young as she. So Gran bought a jar of decaffeinated instant just for Bootsy. Misunderstanding what they were saying, Bootsy called it her *decapitated coffee*. From that time to this, everyone in our family always refers to decaf as *decapitated coffee*. Nor is that an entirely illogical description, it seems to me.

As a child Bootsy spoke with the cutest little lisp. Actually, it was barely discernible, and *lisp* is probably not the exact right term to identify this very minor speech impediment. Imagine, if you can, someone carefully pronouncing every word without allowing the tip of her tongue to lose contact with the back of her front teeth. It is impossible to do this without mispronouncing certain words. But what was adorable in a small child became a monumental embarrassment for a teenager. By high school, Bootsy had become so self-conscious of the way she spoke that she tried never to open her mouth in front of anyone not a family member or a close friend. Talking on the telephone she especially dreaded. Finally, at age nineteen, she consulted a speech therapist, who then referred her to an oral surgeon. It seemed that she had a deformity inside her mouth that did not allow her tongue the freedom of movement it should have. Following an outpatient procedure, she spent countless hours in therapy re-learning how to speak. Curiously, she is still uncomfortable talking on the telephone and does so only with the greatest reluctance. Yet no trace of her former lisp can now be detected.

At age thirteen she taught herself American Sign Language, claiming her primary motive to be a crush she had on the actress Marlee Matlin. But I believe her reason had more to do with awareness of her inability to clearly pronounce certain words. In any case, she eventually made good use of this new skill by signing as a deaf interpreter on television and in a number of video productions.

I suppose I should also mention Bootsy's other insecurity, which has to do with a lazy left eye, the muscles of which don't always want to be bothered to follow the movement of the right eye. It is a genetic trait inherited from Bootsy's natural father. I am unaffected, because my father is not hers. But others of his offspring, including one PA Jalili, about whom I shall have more to say in a later chapter, are similarly afflicted. For years Bootsy wore her hair in a style like that of some old-time movie stars, whereby the left half of the face would be partially obscured by long tresses.

"I should wear a black eye patch," Bootsy told me once as we perused the latest additions to Gran's photo album. "I look like a fucking chameleon."

I tried to reassure her that this not-very-noticeable characteristic in no way detracted from the fact that she was drop-dead gorgeous. But of course, she didn't want to hear it. In her mind, this very minor imperfection was magnified out of all proportion. That was ten years ago. I believe she still sees herself the same way; but at least she seems to have got past obsessing about her looks.

I wonder if perhaps these little insecurities of hers were not a blessing in disguise. In other ways, she is so close to perfect that she might easily have grown up as vain and full of herself as Justin Bieber appears to be. As it is, no one ever has to remind Bootsy that humility is a virtue. It comes naturally to her, and it's one of her most endearing qualities.

Now, let's see. This is tricky, covering ground Bootsy herself has already covered. I have to assume that anyone reading this will have read *Baring All*. But there are numerous details of our childhood that she didn't bother to mention. Or maybe she and I simply recall different incidents.

I remember, for instance, a road trip with Mother and a girlfriend she had at university. Bootsy has no recollection whatever of this woman, whose name, at least for the sake of this narrative, was *Gretchen*. Gretchen was a few years older than Mother and much more smitten with Mother than was Mother with her. But the two of them had fun together and enjoyed many of the same activities. All the way from Arizona to Georgia, Bootsy and I sat in the back seat, giggling under out breath, pretending to be unaware of the fact that Gretchen, riding shotgun whilst Mother drove, couldn't seem to keep her left hand out from under Mother's dress.

Gretchen amused us with funny stories too, and she always had something clever to say. Bootsy and I were invited to call her *Aunt Gretchen*, and I dutifully complied, but Bootsy, for some inexplicable reason, refused. Still, Bootsy did, over and over again, beg Gretchen for the jokes she enjoyed most.

"Tell me again why I'm so hard to talk to," Bootsy would plead. "I forget."

"How can I have a conversation with you?" Gretchen would explode in fake indignation. "You just say one thing and out the other."

Bootsy's laughter would be so infectious that the rest of us, who had long ago tired of the joke, would find ourselves laughing too.

"Gretchen," Bootsy would then say, "I believe you're developing a limp."

"Yeah, I seem to be going lame in my hind leg."

And even though Bootsy had heard the line a hundred times before, she'd laugh till tears ran down her little cheeks.

We visited mission churches and art museums all along the way, as well as whatever other tourist attractions any of us expressed an interest in. We had no agenda and no particular objective in mind; we just drove till half the days we had allotted for the trip had passed; then we turned around and started back toward home.

Somewhere near Atlanta we toured a monastery in a group of perhaps twenty people. A resident monk served as our guide. He showed us their gardens and communal industries (my memory is vague on that detail), but of course, not the individual cells. The property was enormous and seeing it all involved a lot of walking; so we were quite exhausted when we arrived at a scenic little pond surrounded by crude benches. Brother Bernard (I think that was his name) invited us to sit and rest a while. But when we did so, we were suddenly surrounded by a gaggle of geese demanding to be fed. Lots of people still had scraps of sandwiches left from an earlier picnic lunch; so the noisy geese were rewarded. Bootsy, however, was frightened of them, and no one could imagine why. She had been around animals all her life. With horses, goats, sheep, cattle, chickens, cats, and rabbits she was at ease, but these geese terrified her.

"Why?" Gretchen wanted to know. "What do you think they're going to do to you?"

"They might peck me. Look at 'em. They got big ole red peckers." As excited as she was, Bootsy was talking quite loudly. "Anyway, they're ugly. I don't like the looks of those peckers at all."

Everyone in the crowd was quite amused, but also embarrassed and trying hard not to laugh aloud. Even Brother Bernard seemed to be having a difficult time suppressing his confused emotions.

Back in the car, Gretchen said, "I'll never look at peckers quite the same again."

Mother just smiled tolerantly and said, "Shh!"

Bootsy still had no idea what amusement she gave us all that day.

On other occasions, we made similar trips with other friends and paramours of our mother, most of them male. In fact, before our move to

Mexico, Gretchen may have been the only female lover our mother ever had. But she did have female friends and professional associates with whom we spent time.

Marianne Markham was a film-maker, who employed mother as an actress or model on numerous occasions. Marianne and Mother became quite close pals, but never, as far as I know, more than that. Certainly, Marianne did not behave around Mother the way Gretchen did. She didn't touch and fondle Mother in public. And if they ever kissed, it was in private. That is to say, Bootsy and I never saw them kiss. Nor did Marianne ever suggest that we call her *aunt*.

One project she and Mother worked on together involved Marianne's interviewing Mother on camera about nude modeling and then accompanying Mother to an artist's studio, where she filmed Mother disrobing and being posed and then painted by the artist.

Another of Marianne's film projects was focused on the naturist lifestyle, of which Mother claimed to know next to nothing. But Marianne had already gathered the facts and had even rented a cabin for all of us at a nudist resort in

Oregon or Washington; somewhere in the Northwest anyway. Mother, Bootsy, and I were to be the primary subjects, and the rest of the community there would just be background. For about a week we three went totally nude. We shopped in the nude, we swam and ate and napped and played in the nude. The mosquitoes, incidentally, were terrible. Marianne, also quite naked, followed us everywhere with her camera rolling. There was no support crew. A video of that film is still in circulation on the internet.

During that week Mother became quite good friends with another woman, who had two daughters close to Bootsy's and my ages. She invited us to join her the following year at a nude beach in France. At first it seemed doubtful that we should be able to go, but somehow it worked out, and we spent two weeks at Montalivet. All I remember clearly about that vacation was the gloomy grayness of the sky and water, like what you'd expect to encounter in winter, not in early August. I wonder if the sun ever shines there. We never saw it.

Bootsy and I grew up comfortable in our own skins. We have never felt embarrassed by nakedness, our own or anyone else's. But neither have we ever

32

been inclined toward exhibitionism. We have no need to shock or offend that conservative element of society that is so uptight about nudity. Like our mother, we frequently pose for artists and photographers, but only for those we know to share our artistic vision and never for anyone with a cynical or unhealthy outlook. Nor have we ever participated in any project we deemed pornographic or crude. Indeed, we like to believe that the images we pose for have the power to enrich the lives of those who view them and hopefully even to open minds, encourage tolerance, and promote humanistic values. That might, I acknowledge, be asking for a lot, but every picture that either of us has appeared in is, in its own unique way, a celebration of life. &

III
ST PATRICK'S DAY, 2012

On the day before the cave-in, which happened to be St Patrick's Day, Bootsy was in Houston. She had just completed work on the ghost-written memoirs of a well-known personality, who now takes full credit for that book. No problem. That was the agreement all along. Bootsy was generously rewarded for her anonymous contribution. Usually, when she writes, she prefers to be in her own little house behind my home in Mexico City. But for this project she had needed to collaborate closely with the book's subject and author of record.

In any event, by the time the job was complete, Bootsy was more than ready to come to Mexico, where, as I've already mentioned, she meant to give birth to the twins. Eight months pregnant, she was dreading the long, grueling bus trip. Airlines, she had heard, refused to board women as close to term as she was. I cannot say whether this is so or not, but it is what she had been told by a friend, and she believed it to be true. Fortunately, my husband Geoffrey was in Houston on business at that time and offered to allow Bootsy to fly back with him on his company's plane.

The weary travelers arrived in the early evening, just as I was getting Morgan and Madeleine into their pajamas. The girls greeted their father and aunt with hugs and kisses, then very reluctantly trudged upstairs to bed. Geoffrey went up too to take a shower, and I, promising to meet him later in the bedroom, helped Bootsy carry her luggage back to her own little house. I must remember to tell you more about that house later. It's very interesting.

When Geoffrey stepped out of the bathroom, he found me lying naked on our bed. That's how I like to welcome him home. He travels abroad perhaps five or six times a year, and I have no idea what mischief he gets up to whilst he's away, but when he returns, I make his homecoming sweet.

I have often told him that, if he wants to fuck every whore in every city he visits, he has my blessing. All I ask is that he always use protection, that he never put me at risk of contracting a sexually transmitted disease. This he swears to, and I trust him totally. Of course, he's never offered me the same *carte blanche*, but I feel entitled, by the very liberties I allow him, to whatever dalliances I elect to engage in. In actual fact, I am not very promiscuous. But I reserve for myself the right to screw anyone I desire (assuming he wants me too).

I enjoyed numerous affairs before Geoffrey came into my life, none of them even remotely serious, but pleasurable nonetheless. At age sixteen, when I first laid eyes on him—a dreamily handsome young Englishman of about thirty years—my heart was his, and that fact has never changed. I may play around from time to time with other men, but I could only ever be in love with my husband, the father of my two daughters. If he were no longer a part of my life, I cannot imagine how I should ever again feel whole.

For the first seven years of my marriage, I did not once imagined myself sharing pleasure with anyone but him. Oh, I was already encouraging him to be adventurous whenever he was away from home, but somehow it simply did not occur to me to exercise the same privilege, which I knew to be mine.

Then, during the Christmas holidays of 2009, Bootsy, invited into our home an artist friend of hers from Texas, a man named *Leo Madrigal*, whom she herself wrote about in *Dusky Nightshade and the Littler Heathens* and whom she mentioned again briefly in *Baring All*. He is an uncommonly nice man—charming, talented, and ever-so-wise—the author of an amazing book, *Observations and Contemplations of a Humanist*, which had not yet seen print at the time I first knew him. Leo has painted Bootsy's naked likeness several times, and when he asked me to sit for him, I was delighted to say yes.

I have posed nude for scores of artists and photographers. It's an occupation I enjoy. But I could not have imagined how sexually aroused I was to become during the course of this particular sitting. Leo didn't flirt or make suggestive remarks. He was a perfect gentleman, respectful of me at all times. I cannot begin to explain the way I felt. Bootsy has told me she always has the same experience with Leo. Neither of us believe it to be a clever seduction method he's worked out; but if we're wrong, he should patent it. It's worth a million dollars. Men all over the world would give their entire fortunes for it.

When Leo announced that our first sitting was at an end, the only thing I could think to say was, "I hope to hell you have some condoms in your wallet."

"I do in fact." He laughed self-consciously. "I'm not an optimist by nature, but I believe in being prepared just in case."

That was almost four years ago. I've sat for Leo several times since then, and we always conclude our painting sessions with an exciting and refreshing episode of wholesome, recreational sex. I never feel guilty afterward. I feel exhilarated and empowered. I feel like I could conquer the world.

I have neglected to tell Geoffrey about this till now. Maybe I should have done, but somehow I consider these occasions with Leo as "me time," private and personal, like the hours I spend at the day spa. Of course, in preparing this manuscript, I've had to bring Geoffrey up to speed on all my extramarital activities. I couldn't have him learn of them for the first time after the book comes out. I have to say, he's showed remarkable grace. If he's upset or disappointed with me in the least, he has managed to conceal the fact admirably. I think I'm falling in love with him all over again.

Now, I seem to have digressed from the particular narrative with which I began this chapter, and I don't quite know how to find my way back. Please bear with me; I'm not the professional writer my sister is. If you recall, I was telling you about the night before the accident, the night Bootsy and Geoffrey flew in together from Houston.

Post coitus, Geoffrey and I showered together. Then Geoffrey, totally exhausted from his trip, crawled back into bed and promptly fell sound asleep. I slipped on a beach cover-up and went downstairs to find Bootsy swimming laps naked in our pool. She was as high as someone on amphetamines.

Mind you, my sister never uses recreational drugs of any kind, unless we count caffeine, which is her only chemical vice. Except for coffee, she lives an absolutely pure life (substance-wise anyway). Her highs are inevitably the natural result of some victory or accomplishment.

I threw off my garment, dove in, and swam with her till we were both too tired to continue. Then floating on our backs and gazing up at the night sky, we talked for hours the way we had as children, sharing all our most-intimate secrets. Her exultant mood tonight was the effect of an experience she had had on the flight home.

"Geoffrey and I weren't the only passengers. There were six other men, big-shot corporate executives, by the look of them, not the kind of guys I should ordinarily find very interesting, but intelligent and well-dressed. I do like both those qualities. Anyway, when Geoffrey bragged to them that I was a published author, they asked me to read them a selection from one of my books, which, of course, I had a copy of in my carry-on. I began by reading them that paragraph in *Baring All* about my fondness for sex. It's got to be one of the best things I've ever written. Immediately, I had their full attention.

They begged me to read more; so I started over at the beginning of Chapter I, and at their continued urging, I kept reading till the plane landed. They loved me, Dusty. They were mesmerized. Do you have any idea how gratifying that is?"

I laughed. "A pretty girl speaking candidly about sexual matters: what would you expect?"

"Well, sex is what interests me. I can't think of any other subject more worthy of being written about."

"Maybe you'll get some book sales out of this?"

"Oh, yeah, definitely. I should carry extra copies. I had to suggest that they order from Amazon, but I told them, if they brought their books here, I'd sign them. I hope that's okay."

"Of course."

For a while then we floated in silence. From behind a cloud the waning quarter moon appeared. There were no stars to be seen, even when the clouds had completely cleared away. In our childhood at the ranch in Arizona the sky had been strewn with stars. Where did they all go?

"I learned something about myself tonight," Bootsy mused. "On the flight down, I mean."

"What's that?"

"That I quite like being desired."

"Everybody wants to be wanted. Who desired you tonight that so pleased you?"

"All of them. Every man on that plane." Then, remembering to whom she was speaking, she added, "Except your husband, of course. He only has eyes for you."

I knew better than that, of course.

"You should have been there, Dusty. The atmosphere was so sexually charged it was like electricity crackling in the air. I could taste it, smell it, feel it. I'll bet you anything they all had erections."

"Sure, they all wanted to fuck you. I'm not surprised. But are you telling me that their excitement infected you? Did they make you want to fuck them?"

"No, there's not one of them I'd ever want to have sex with. But I was affected nonetheless, and in a way that was almost (but not quite) sexual. I mean, I was excited by awareness of their wanting me, but not in a way that made me want them. Does that make any sense at all?"

"I think so. They made you feel important, validated, valued."

"More like worshiped and adored. But I'm not heartless. I didn't want them tormented with unsatisfied longing. If I'd had the nerve and if Geoffrey weren't amongst them, I'd like to have found a way to get them off without actually having them inside me."

"Fellatio?"

"No, no. Never. To me sucking seems even more intimate than fucking. I mean, they'd still be inside me. But maybe I could have given them all hand jobs. I'd do that for almost anybody that's not an absolute creep. It doesn't feel like a violation of my person."

"Well, then, next time just go for it. And if Geoffrey's present, you have my permission to include him. Hell, you can fuck him if you ever want to."

"I don't. I mean, he's cute and all. I can easily see what you like about him, but he's not my type. I could never be in love with him. And I really do have to be very deeply in love with someone to want his penis inside me."

The following morning at breakfast, Bootsy asked me to make a few snapshots of her. She hated the way she looked pregnant and had, since starting to show, avoided appearing in any photos, save in a few anonymous studio nudes by Sebastian Drake. But now a number of her friends overseas were begging to see her as a mother-to-be, and she couldn't bear to say no to them. Thanks be to God (Whom we don't believe in) Morgan and Madeleine didn't follow us outside. While I carried only my camera-equipped cell phone, Bootsy carried her coffee mug. We walked across the patio and through the gate into Bootsy's back garden. She posed in front of a gardenia bush, and I framed her image in my screen. The only warning we had before the earth opened up and swallowed us was a brief trembling beneath our feet. ๛

IV
PRIMROSE COTTAGE

Bootsy calls her little house *Primrose Cottage*, the reason being that when Geoffrey and I deeded it to her a few years ago, the interior throughout was covered with wallpaper featuring primroses. The house itself, one of the oldest European structures in Mexico, had come into our possession when we bought an out-of-business boutique hotel, which we intended to remodel as our home. The two lots adjoined and were offered for sale together, but we had no use whatever for the little house, which had once been home to the hotel manager. Its small kitchen garden communicated with the hotel patio by way of an ornate ironwork gate. So we gave the smaller property to Bootsy, hoping that she would choose to live there. I liked the idea of having my sister close to me, and Geoffrey likes to see me happy; so he offered no objection when I suggested that we make it a graduation gift when Bootsy received her first university degree.

The original structure consisted of two small rooms (10′ x 10′ each) with a wide arched doorway between. These rooms Bootsy uses as living room and bedroom. Across the back of the house, a board-and-batten extension had been added during the late nineteenth century. This extension gives the house a tiny kitchen directly behind the living room and a bathroom adjoining the bedroom. Around 1900 the house had been wired for electricity, but the exposed wiring was in such terrible condition that Bootsy immediately tore it out. I imagine she meant to rewire promptly, but somehow she always had other projects of higher priority. For years she used the house without electricity.

The original adobe-and-rubble walls are some thirty inches thick. The front door is a crude and massive hardwood affair with hinges and strap reinforcements of wrought iron. The only windows in the front part of the house are mere rifle slits. Glass has been added, but the windows don't open. There is no front garden. The main door opens directly onto the sidewalk. For security reasons Bootsy never uses that door. She always comes and goes through our house or else through a postern on a busy and well-lit side street.

Her kitchen has four good-size windows looking out on her own back garden, where she grows herbs. She's not much of a cook, but she loves the scent of rosemary, basil, thyme, mint, and oregano. Everything she has planted there is heavily scented. Along the wall that separates our two properties, she has put in gardenia bushes.

But Bootsy doesn't actually live here. She considers Houston her primary home. Primrose Cottage is her retreat from the world. It is where she writes. And by preference, she usually composes her books on a manual typewriter. There's a story behind that, but she's already told it herself in a little hand-bound book entitled *Foreign Affairs*. So I shan't go into it any further.

Bootsy rewired Primrose Cottage earlier this year, scraped off all the wallpaper and painted the inside with colors reminiscent of the desert Southwest, where she and I were born. It is a lovely house now, but barely large enough for one person (300 square feet total). She never entertains there. I doubt that any of her lovers, save Percy

Cabot and Cricket Firestone, have ever seen the inside.

So private is this tiny house that Bootsy can afford never to wear clothes at home during warm weather. Nor does she have a telephone. When I need to communicate with her, I either walk there myself or I send one of my daughters to deliver a message. Recently, I sent Madeleine, my eleven-year-old, to invite Bootsy to join us on the patio for home-made ice cream. Madeleine found her aunt quite naked at her laptop, deeply absorbed in a chat with one of her many Facebook friends. The invitation was made and accepted. Then whilst Bootsy got dressed, Madeleine perused the computer screen, which Bootsy had inadvertently left open.

"Your friend," Madeleine informed her aunt as they prepared to leave the house together, "is not a very good speller. She spelled *come* c-u-m."

Before the twins were born, Bootsy often spent no more than a few weeks out of the year at Primrose Cottage. But now that she has daughters to visit, she cannot seem to stay away. She travels to Houston or Bagdad or somewhere else for just a few weeks at a time, then returns to us for a month or more before

48

going off on another adventure, which never lasts for long.

Whenever she is in residence, she is fond of outings at Bosque de Chapultepec, Mexico City's equivalent to New York City's Central Park. There are walking trails, scenic lakes, a magnificent old castle, museums, outdoor statuary, and best of all, a splendid zoo. Together, the two of us often take picnics at this park with our four little girls and our mother.

And every weekend just about we visit the Bazaar Sábado, which is within easy walking distance of our houses. On two adjacent plazas local artists and native craftsmen display their paintings, handmade baskets, blown glass, wood-work, pottery, textiles, masques, dolls, costume jewelry, religious icons, and figurines. Oh, yes, there are always lots of flowers for sale at the Bazaar Sábado too. And live music is free, unless you feel like leaving a gratuity. In the central building (actually an elegant old mansion) is a restaurant, where we usually stop for *antojitos* (hot snack foods) and beverages.

My sister has never been very domestic. Indeed, it has always seemed to me that she took some kind of perverse pride in not knowing how to cook even the simplest foods. However, since the birth of the twins, she has made a sincere effort to learn not only the basics of the culinary art, but also to memorize as many recipes as possible. As she says it, "I still feel awkward in the kitchen, but at least, I'm no longer a total stranger there. And if the girls ever have to depend on me, they won't starve."

Bootsy has never enjoyed permanent full-time employment. She prefers not to make that kind of commitment. She seeks, instead, temporary short-term assignments. Periodically she conducts creative writing seminars, and seasonally, she teaches salsa in the Zona Rosa. Of course, she also sells her artworks, craft items, and jewelry online at Etsy and at Amazon. While she doesn't make a lot of money at this, her business is steadily picking up. The same is true of her book and photography royalties. I'm terribly impressed at how easily she seems to manage without a job. If she stresses at all about money, she never allows me to know it. Nor does she ever ask me or anyone else to help her out financially.

Bootsy lives elegantly but not extravagantly. She has a driver's license, but she has never owned a vehicle.

Every two or three years, when I get a new car (always a Jaguar saloon), I offer Bootsy my old one free of charge, but she inevitably declines, citing her reluctance to take on the responsibility of insuring and maintaining a vehicle. She travels a lot, to be sure, but usually by bus, which is the most economical means by far. She still models for painters and sculptors, but no longer for photographers or videographers. Since the accident, she has not the self-confidence. Her looks are recovering slowly, but she remains uncertain of her photogeneity.

She should, it seems to me, be reassured by the number of heads she turns and the compliments she receives from total strangers. But then she has never allowed the opinions of others to mean that much to her. Mind you, she does not belittle or deny the compliments that are offered her, but receives them graciously and always remembers to say thank you, even when the compliments are inappropriate or crudely phrased. Here's an example of what I'm talking about:

"Ooh! Nice tits, Mama," this from a teenage boy at a bus stop in Phoenix.

Many women would have taken umbrage, as I'm sure I should have done myself, but not our Bootsy. "Oh, thanks," she said offhandedly. "I've had 'em since I was twelve."

On another occasion—I think we were shopping at the Galleria in Houston—she was similarly complimented on her shapely behind. "Lady, I hope you don't take this the wrong way, but I have to tell you. You got just about the cutest ass I ever saw."

"So glad you like it," she told her admirer, a young soldier in uniform. "It's from Jenny Craig."

One of the mottoes by which Bootsy lives is never to take offense unless offense is intended. If workmen whistle at her as she passes by a construction site, she generously chooses to believe that they are paying her a heartfelt compliment, and she rewards them with a little wave. "It costs me nothing, and it seems to please them. So why not?"

By age eight Bootsy had determined that writing would be her profession. By age eighteen she had made up her mind to become famous. "If I hope to get people to read what I write, then they first have to know who I am and find me interesting. Other than for that purpose, fame would have no appeal for me whatever."

And insomuch as Bootsy is always successful at whatever she sets out to accomplish, she fully expects someday to be famous. With that in mind and hoping to protect her future privacy and that of all her family, she never shares with anyone our addresses or phone numbers in Mexico or Arizona. She interacts with the world only through the Griffoun Society in Houston. Her studio in the Griffoun Clubhouse is open to the public whether she happens to be there or not. If she is away, some other member can show her artworks or sell signed copies of her books. ∽

V

THE VILLAGE OF MERRYMEAD

Mexico's Federal District, with a total population of close to nine million, is comprised of sixteen boroughs (or *delegaciones*). My house and Bootsy's house next door are situated in the Borough of Álvaro Obregón, which is commonly referred to as *Villa Obregón*. Our mother lives in the next borough to the east of us, Coyoacán. Some boroughs are considerably larger than others. Villa Obregón, while not one of the largest boroughs, is elongated and comprised of more than one neighborhood (or *barrio*), our own neighborhood being San Ángel. Coyoacán, on the other hand, is one of the smallest boroughs. Its primary *barrio* is also named *Coyoacán*. San Ángel and Coyoacán together constitute Mexico City's historic district, comparable in charm to Georgetown in the District of Columbia. These are upscale neighborhoods with cobblestone streets, colonial churches, and beautiful old mansions surrounded by lush tropical gardens only partially obscured by high brick walls.

Bootsy was twelve and I was sixteen the year we first saw Mexico City. Our mother brought us here on vacation and we decided to stay. Our first home was in the Delegación Cuauhtémoc in a spacious apartment above a Zona Rosa art gallery managed by our mother. The Zona Rosa, by the way, is Mexico City's tourist district, where all the poshest hotels, restaurants, and gift shops are located.

We arrived early in the summer. In September we were enrolled at an English-language girls' boarding school in Coyoacán. This school was operated by very nice family of Canadians. Bootsy and I were the only American students that year. The other girls, save one Japanese and one Mexican, were all English. British spelling was the standard, and consequently, I still have trouble remembering to write *program*, instead of *programme*, or *labor*, instead of *labour*. I imagine it's even harder for Bootsy than for me, since she was younger than I when she started there and attended for more years than did I.

We boarded for just one year. Sweetbrier Seminary for Young Ladies of Quality (the founder and headmaster had a lovely sense of ~~humour~~ humor, don't you think?) had beds for but thirteen girls. In order for the school to expand, it became necessary to begin accepting day students. So for our second year, Bootsy and I became two of the first five scholars not to live on campus.

Mother had but recently bought an apartment building a few blocks from our school. She had also left her job at the art gallery in favor of an editorial position at *The Daily News*, an English-language periodical much respected throughout Mexico. So now we moved into the manager's unit on the ground floor of our new apartment building. Every morning Bootsy and I walked to school together. Our route took us right by Frida Kahlo's Blue House, which is now a museum.

In December I graduated, and in January I wed. Bootsy continued at Sweetbrier for two and a half more years, graduating about two weeks before her sixteenth birthday. But I seem to be getting ahead of myself. I wanted to tell you about some of the tenants and goings-on in Mother's building.

Beatriz Jara, usually called *Bea* (pronounced Bay-uh), was fourteen years old (halfway between Bootsy's age and mine) when she came to work for us as our housekeeper. She earned only a pittance to begin with; but we really did not need a housekeeper. Mother hired her simply because Bea seemed so desperate for a job. This was whilst we were still in the apartment over the art gallery. And because Bea did not wish to live at home, where, apparently, she was treated rather shabbily, Mother fixed her a bed in our laundry room. I suppose Mother was the first person ever to have shown Bea any kindness, for Bea quickly came to worship Mother. Bea's loyalty was fierce and absolute. Well, for that matter, it still is. She and Mother are lovers now. They have been for some years. In any event, when we moved to Coyoacán, Bea went with us and got a real bedroom of her own. Of course, after Bootsy graduated from university and went away to Texas to pursue further degrees, Bea was invited to share the master bedroom with Mother. They make a lovely couple, and Bootsy and I are happy for them both.

The only other apartment on the ground floor of that building belongs to an elderly widow known to Bootsy and me only as *señora Gomez*. She speaks no English. Her constant companion is a rebarbative little Chihuahua dog called *Pepe*. Pepe seems to hate everyone in the world, except *señora* Gomez, whom he adores. And she, of course, adores him. She allows him to get away with barking and growling at anyone who comes near. She doesn't even scold him if he bites at people's ankles. And our mother is so fond of this old lady that she chooses also to ignore the bad behavior of the dog, which seems to dislike Bootsy above everyone else in the world.

On our very first encounter with this rude little Chihuahua, Bootsy exclaimed in English, "How cute is that? She's trained her rat to bark like a dog."

Mother and I, in spite of ourselves, laughed aloud. Naturally, *señora* Gomez wanted to know what Bootsy had said. I should certainly have lied, but Mother chose to faithfully render Bootsy's remark into Spanish. *Señora* Gomez was steamed, to be sure, but she eventually forgave Mother and me for laughing. However, she has never forgiven Bootsy the remark. Nor has Bootsy ever offered an apology. As far as I know, *señora* Gomez is my sister's only enemy. No, I take it back There is another: the wife of one of her paramours.

Other tenants of the building included artists and writers, most of them British expatriates. During our first few years there, Mother, Bootsy, and I each posed for all the artists in our building and for others in our immediate neighborhood. Coyoacán is something of a Mecca for painters, photographers, and others in creative fields.

As Bootsy and I came to realize how populous was the English-speaking community in that part of Mexico City, we privately renamed our neighborhood *Merrymead*, for we found it easy to imagine ourselves in a quaint little hamlet in the English countryside. Bootsy, of course, is the one who came up with the new name, suggested, no doubt, by Agatha Christi, whose fictional crime solver Miss Marple hailed from the village of St Mary Mead. We even had, in the person of Solomon Thorn, a lord of the manor, his grand home appropriately called the *Brambles*.

Fabulously wealthy, Solomon Thorn was (and is) the unchallenged leader of the community of Brits in Coyoacán and San Ángel. He had, a few years earlier, donated the land and buildings that housed our school. His own niece, Salome Thorn, was a classmate of mine, and it had been specifically for her benefit that the school had been established. A self-described "remittance man," Solomon had come to Mexico in the wake of some unspeakable scandal during the 1960s, and had never returned to England. Instead, he had sought citizenship here and invested in real estate. He owns dozens, if not hundreds, of rental properties in the Federal District. For a while, he courted our mother, but I cannot say whether they ever became lovers.

I do know that when Mother told him how Bootsy and I referred to the English-speaking community within San Ángel-Coyoacán, he was hugely amused. He embraced the name *Merrymead* and encouraged its widespread use. Of course, the name is still quite unofficial and appears on no map. But many of those who live here are proud to tell you that they reside in the Village of Merrymead. Salome and her girlfriend Daphne Trent edit a community newsletter entitled *The Merrymead Reporter*, which comes out at irregular intervals, usually about every two weeks. Bootsy and I have both contributed articles, poetry, and crossword puzzles to this periodic publication. ❧

VI
THE GRIFFOUN YEARS

Bootsy, having finished high school at age fifteen, graduated from National Autonomous University here in Mexico City just a couple of weeks before her eighteenth birthday. She then said goodbye to us all and traveled to Austin, Texas, to pursue advanced degrees in literature. An old friend from Arizona, Damien Wynter, was already living in the Austin area and introduced Bootsy to the Griffoun Society, a cooperative association of artists and writers with a clubhouse just off the main University of Texas campus.

61

The Griffoun Society, in those days, had a very attractive volunteer program, whereby eight young ladies were offered luxury living accommodations in exchange for their commitment to pose regularly for life classes sponsored by the club. Volunteers were also expected to spend a few hours each week serving as towel girls and attendants in the club's spa and gymnasium or to serve refreshments in an alcohol-free pub on the ground floor of the clubhouse.

Applications for these coveted positions had to be made on video. Typically fifty to a hundred girls applied every summer. Rarely were there more than two or three positions open at that time, for once chosen, a girl could expect to keep her place as long as she wanted it (usually until graduation).

The clubhouse boasted five stories plus a finished-out basement. The volunteers' dormitory was on the uppermost floor. On the ground floor were a used-book exchange, a laundromat, the Griffoun Society library and reading room, and the pub already mentioned. The floors in between were devoted to a spa and gymnasium, cooperative studios (painting, etching, photography, videography, ceramics, stained glass, and sculpture), and a couple of classrooms, where creative-writing seminars and other workshops were conducted. The basement housed a banquet facility.

Napoleon Plum, a Griffoun Society insider, directed Bootsy's video application. "We're looking for a run time of about three minutes. We can do as many takes as necessary to get it right. So don't be nervous. The primary responsibility of a Griffoun volunteer is to pose nude for art classes. So I'm going to ask you to undress on camera. And as you do so, I want you to tell me about yourself: your full name, your age, your birth date, your interests and ambitions, anything you want the selection committee to be aware of. Just keep talking till I signal you. Then wrap it up as tidily as you can. And don't forget to do a turn-around so we can see you from all angles."

Napoleon was so pleased with Bootsy's first take that he did not even bother to do a second one. "You'll be notified in August if you've made the cut. But I don't think you need to worry about it. I've never seen anyone more natural. You're a shoe-in."

The following week Napoleon drove Bootsy to Houston in order to introduce her to the artist Percy Cabot. Bootsy had owned an etching by Percy since she was a little girl, and she was mad to meet him in person. I suppose it must have been love at first sight, because Bootsy said she knew almost immediately that Percy was destined to be the most important person in her life. She flirted and teased and did everything she could think of to let him know how she felt. But Percy, being forty-three years older than she, could hardly believe that she was serious.

"See here," he said at last. "If you're not an heiress nymphomaniac with a preference for men of your grandfather's generation, you should tell me now, lest the disappointment later on be too much for me to bear."

"Sorry; I'm destitute."

From September of 2004 until December of 2009, Bootsy's world was comprised of three parts: the UT campus, the Griffoun Society clubhouse, and Percy's art studio and apartment in Houston. She commuted by Greyhound between Austin and Houston.

Posing for drawing classes, she tells me, is a lot harder work and considerably less enjoyable than the kind of modeling she was used to. But then she also had the opportunity to earn cash money doing sittings of the kind she likes best (posing for member artists and photographers whom she met through the club). She considers her years as a Griffoun Society volunteer the most-rewarding and carefree time of her life.

Bootsy especially enjoyed working in the pub, and while she wasn't paid a salary, she was able to earn good tips. During the fall semester of her first year in Austin, I visited her there. We had never before been separated for more than a few days, and I missed her almost unendurably.

I arrived in Austin on a Friday afternoon, but by the time I checked into a hotel, showered, and changed clothes, the evening was well underway. I found Bootsy waiting tables in the crowded pub. *Amazing!* I thought to myself. *They don't even serve alcohol here. How can they attract such crowds?*

I sat down at a recently vacated table for two, and Bootsy, in safari clothes, hurried over to embrace me and welcome me to Texas. Then she grabbed a damp bar towel and wiped the table for me. Her loose-fitting blouse was undone to the fourth button and gaping . As usual, she was wearing no bra. I started to warn her that, were she not careful, she'd be treating someone to a good look at her boobies.

"Shh!" she said with a wink and a smile. "That's the secret of my success. These guys don't come in here for the Near Beer."

The other two waitresses on duty, Bambi Nguyen and Dana Mars, were similarly attired in brown cotton skits with cargo pockets, sneakers, white safari blouses, khaki photojournalists' vests, and fedoras reminiscent of Indiana Jones. It was a cute uniform, and the occasional glimpse I got of a pink nipple seemed entirely accidental. Sex sells, I guess. They were doing here exactly what places like Hooters is notorious for doing, but they were doing it with more finesse, which somehow makes the whole business a lot less objectionable. At least to my thinking.

Snack foods were available (*tapas*, nuts, chips, pickled eggs, that sort of thing) but no sandwiches or hot food. Beverages included six brands of non-alcoholic beer and ale, as well as several labels of alcohol-free wines sold only by the bottle. The wine rack behind the bar reached all the way to the ceiling, the most expensive wines being at the top.

Whenever a bottle was ordered, the waitress had to go up the ladder for it. I watched each of the girls go up and down several times. They all wore the scantiest thong panties imaginable. Very clever! All the wine sold that night was from the upper reaches.

At the bar Bootsy had a group of wine-drinkers that she was waiting on. As she climbed the ladder for them the first time, she said, "Now, don't you guys look up my skirt."

They gallantly assured her that they'd never do such a despicable thing. But then they made a spectacle of themselves craning their necks to get a better view. Bootsy just laughed.

The second time that same bunch sent her up the ladder, she said, "I think you guys just like to look at my panties. I'll bet you don't even like wine."

Their protestations of innocence sounded very hollow to me.

Later, on her third trip up the ladder, she said, "I'm going to surprise you all one of these day and not even wear panties. Then we'll see how much you really like wine."

"Just take them off now," one of the boys urged her.

"I dare you," said another.

A third had a more-helpful suggestion. "All you girls who work here should put your panties up for auction some night. I'll bet you could make a mint if you'd let the winner take 'em off of you."

"Mmm! I'll have to run that by the management. I shouldn't want the police to shut us down."

I never heard whether that auction eventually took place or not.

Now, before I close this chapter, I want to tell you about one other incident that occurred during Bootsy's tenure as a Griffoun volunteer. Remember, she was, at the time, pursuing first an MA and then a PhD. She was a full-time student.

One night, leaving the library late, she started across the campus toward the nearest gate on Guadalupe Street and was accosted by a group of six obnoxiously inebriated undergraduate men, who surrounded her, making lewd remarks and taking liberties with her person. There is no telling how far this might have gone had not Napoleon Plum happen by.

At that time Napoleon was about forty years of age. He wasn't obese or obviously out of shape, but he certainly didn't look like anyone to be reckoned with. His polite suggestion that the boys go on back to their frat house and sleep it off was met with obscene verbal abuse, which quickly escalated to a physical attack. In less than thirty seconds, however, using only one hand (he was carrying a camera case in his left hand and neither dropped it nor put it down) and his feet, he vanquished all six of his opponents, then offered Bootsy his arm and escorted her back to the dormitory.

"Napoleon was definitely my hero that night," Bootsy told me at Christmas. "Who would have guessed that he used to be a martial-arts competitor with scads of trophies. It was just like in a Chuck Norris movie."

Napoleon was never to be Bootsy's lover, however. She simply couldn't make herself feel that way about him. No matter. Dana Mars was eager to put her brand on him. ∞

VII
PERCY CABOT

I have already mentioned Percy Cabot, but his importance in Bootsy's life is so great that I feel I must say a bit more about him and about Bootsy's relationship with him. I know for a fact that she proposed to him, rather than he to her, this when she was only eighteen years old. Whether they are truly married or not is, I suppose, a matter of opinion. There was a ceremony, to be sure (a Navajo house blessing actually), but there was no license. The County Clerk's Office in Houston has no record of a marriage between Percy Cabot and Trudy Silverheels. Nor has Bootsy ever taken Percy's last name. But she and he did exchange rings, and I know that she considers him her soul mate, but whether she counts him as her husband is somewhat unclear.

Their relationship, though very close, is certainly unconventional. Neither of them makes any pretense of being faithful to the other. And yet the two of them exhibit uncommon loyalty and devotion to each other. To observe them together is quite inspirational. Percy calls their relationship an *open marriage*. Bootsy's term for it is *casual, non-exclusive monogamy*. However, they do not even live together, except for about four months out of the year. On various social-media sites, Bootsy's relationship status is listed as *single*. I think it would be more honest of her to check the box marked *It's complicated*. She and Percy have been a number for nine years now and seem no less in love today than they were in the beginning.

They share ownership of an art studio and wood shop. Percy established this atelier single-handedly decades ago, but Bootsy, since becoming his partner, has enlarged it and added new capabilities every year. At age seventy, Percy is pretty much retired, except to support Bootsy's career. She is the primary one to make use of the shop and studio these days. He answers the phones, takes orders, and keeps the books.

To market her creations and those of other members of the Griffoun Society, she established an online outlet. Initially Silverheels Trading Post was an eStore but, when it became apparent that she could sell more goods through Etsy and Amazon than through her own site, Bootsy did away with her shopping carts and expanded the site's purely informational features, the focus being on Native American culture. Handcrafted goods are displayed, as in a traditional trading post, but buyers are referred either to Etsy or Amazon.

After the Griffoun Society clubhouse in Austin burned to the ground at the end of 2009, it seemed for a while as if the club would cease to exist. But Bootsy, a former volunteer and new member herself, refused to allow that to happen. She contacted Simon Estes, who had been the club's managing director since 1967, and with his blessing, she built a Griffoun Society website and began organizing support to re-establish the Griffoun Society in Houston, where she now lived and worked.

In 2010 Christi Broughton, recently divorced from Randy Nakamura, was living in Houston and in the same building with Percy and Bootsy. Christi is the publisher at Griffoun Press, which is the dedicated publishing company for the Griffoun Society. Incidentally, Christi has known Percy since she was a child. In 2010 Randy was the Griffoun Society's art director. He has a house at Lake Travis just outside of Austin. Apparently his divorce from Christi was an amicable one, for he and she worked together to help re-start the Griffoun Society.

Christi is the person responsible for persuading Bootsy to write *Dusky Nightshade and the Little Heathens*, which happens to be the true story of a Griffoun Society member, Leo Madrigal. Leo's own book *Observations and Contemplations of a Humanist* had just been published earlier that year (2010).

"If you'll tell his story, Griffoun Press will produce it and see that it gets published," Christi promised.

In fact, Bootsy had played a small part in the events she was being asked to write about. Little or no research would be required. She was already in possession of all the pertinent facts. And writing is what she does best and loves the most. The project required about two months, which time Bootsy spent holed up in Primrose Cottage, where she could work without distraction.

Christi, meanwhile, was expanding Griffoun Press, adding two new production imprints: Summer Snow Scriptorium and Pouty Poppet Press. The imprint that would be associated with *Dusky Nightshade and the Little Heathens* was to be Summer Snow Scriptorium. Pouty Poppet Press would be reserved for children's books.

By the autumn of 2011, Christi and Randy had remarried, and Christi had moved back to Austin. As for Bootsy, she was once more ensconced in Primrose Cottage, working, this time, on a fictionalized erotic memoir to be entitled *Baring All*. After publication of her first novel, she had returned to Houston, and pumped up with the excitement of her literary success, she had been extremely productive in the studio. She now had dozens of artworks ready to show, and Percy was actively seeking a gallery interested in handling her art.

In November Bootsy, four and a half months pregnant with the twins, was actually typing the final chapter of *Baring All* when I took a call for her from Percy. He had arranged for her and him to be in an art show together in the Montrose neighborhood (the arts district) of Houston. It was a two-day exhibition scheduled for the first weekend in December. Was there any way she could make it back in time?

"Sure. I'm almost finished here," she told him. "I'll be there with bells on."

On the twenty-fourth day of November, 2011, *Baring All* was published, and Bootsy set out by autobus for Houston. She was there in plenty of time for the art show, but fainted dead away on the morning of the opening and could not immediately be revived. She was rushed to hospital and spent the entire weekend undergoing tests. Eventually she was released with a warning not to get too tired out. It was assumed, I think, that her pregnancy was somehow to blame.

Then shortly after the first of the year, Bootsy was in Dallas to do a public reading from her novel and afterward to autograph some books. Half way through her presentation, she just keeled over, toppling her lectern in dramatic fashion. She was again rushed to hospital and once more underwent a battery of tests. No specific diagnosis was ever determined, but the consensus seemed to be that her pregnancy must be behind this troubling tendency of hers to fall suddenly into unconsciousness.

Then the cave-in occurred in March, and for months afterward, Bootsy was in hospital or in therapy as an outpatient. The next time she suffered a fainting spell was in December of 2012, exactly a year after the first occurrence. This time there was no pregnancy to cite as a possible cause. It was, of course, a big temptation to think this latest event was related to the head trauma she had incurred last spring. But the fact that she had previously passed out this way twice before the accident forced the doctors to take this a bit more seriously. They subjected her to every test imaginable, and yet the reason behind her fainting continues to confound them.

I worry still about Bootsy's health, as do Mother, Gran, Michelle, and Percy. It is so unlike her to be ill. I only ever recall her being sick once in her life, and that was when she was about seven years old. Oh, she's endured injuries and broken bones. She is active and adventurous, after all, but she's never had a weak constitution. I don't quite

know what else to say about this. It is a
mystery and a very troubling one at that.

᭖

VIII
RODEO SEX

Nobody is a better storyteller than my sister. She doesn't just say the words; she treats her listener to a dramatic experience so rich it seems almost real. I think she would be a fantastic actress. She could stand on an otherwise empty stage and speak for two solid hours, and her audience would be absolutely enthralled.

A few years ago, she interviewed a man who had spent years on death row and wanted her to tell his story. He had but recently been released from prison and was residing temporarily at the Ben Reid Halfway House in Houston. She visited him there a few times, but eventually decided, for a number of reasons, not to ghost-write his book for him. However, during the course of those interviews, he regaled her with a funny description of what he called *rodeo sex*. It's a discourse she likes to repeat whenever she can find a fresh audience for it. And the moment she opens her mouth to speak, she seems actually to become that old ex-convict himself.

"Rodeo sex ain't a lot different from regular sex, at least to start with. But you kin only do it once with each gal. The important thang is put it off till yer startin' to git kind bored with her and yer looking to move on anyway. But don't let on. Not even a little. If fact, to set it up right, you gotta be extra sweet and sensitive-like. Get duded up fer her and brang her flowers, maybe even take her out to dinner someplace fancy. That'll cost a heap, but the experience is gonna be worth it. You kin take my word fer that. Tell her how purty she is and compliment things you don't really even give a shit about. And don't rush her like you usually do. You gotta make sure she's really in the mood. Then you just ease it in as gentle as you kin, saying all the tenderest words you kin thank of. Take yer time, and when she's really getting into it, lean down close and whisper in her ear, 'I love you.' But call her by another gal's name. Pardner, if you kin stay in the saddle fer eight seconds, yer a real cowboy."

Bobby, the guy who first told Bootsy about rodeo sex had once been within minutes of being put to death. Strapped in the electric chair, he had been made to immerse his bare feet in buckets of water. A last minute reprieve had saved his life, and eventually his death sentence had been commuted to life in prison. After four more decades he had been paroled. And that's when Bootsy had been asked to tell his story. The law would not have permitted him to profit financially from the sale of his book, and he understood that. He simply wanted to be heard. Bootsy referred him to someone else, another writer she knows through the Griffoun Society. ∾

IX
OLD JUPITER

At the ranch in Arizona, our grandmother used to have a stallion that was a particularly valuable source of income. The foals it sired were splendid animals, but Old Jupiter himself was the most-inept stud anyone can imagine. Clients brought their mares to him from all over the Southwest, but every engagement gave us cause to worry that the desired coupling would not take place and we'd have to return the fee.

Gran's foreman Jake was totally contemptuous of Old Jupiter. "He's a goddam klutz of the type that, were he a man, couldn't get laid in a whorehouse."

The problem was never that Old Jupiter lacked interest in the mares. It was more the opposite problem. He was easily aroused, but the more excited he got, the less able he seemed to find his mark. The ranch has a special breeding pen constructed of heavy timber. Into that pen we would lead a mare, then let Old Jupiter in behind her. The mare was trapped and couldn't wander off, even if she got bored with Old Jupiter's awkward attempts to mate with her. She just had to stand there and suffer his clumsiness, and yet the outcome was always doubtful.

On one occasion Bootsy, meaning to help Old Jupiter achieve penetration, reached through the fence to grasp his turgid member, but she was not immediately able to guide it home, for the reason that he was lunging about so wildly. Still, Bootsy was determined. Holding on firmly, she tugged and pulled. Had Old Jupiter just trusted her to do right by him, she would have made the connection in a jiff. But he seemed to be working against her (and thus against himself).

Gran, terrified for Bootsy's safety, ran from the porch, screaming for her to let go and get back. The client, a fat, middle-age rancher from Utah was holding his sides laughing. In that moment Old Jupiter ejaculated all over the mare's back. Horses come by the cupful, if not by the pint. One good-size glob struck Bootsy on the cheek, but she was unaware of it until the dust settled and I could tell her to wipe her face.

Gran was livid. I have never seen her so upset. But the mare's owner said no problem. He'd simply let us board the mare overnight and we could try again in the morning. He wouldn't take anything for the experience of having seen "that little slip of a girl jerk off a stallion." ∞

X
PRETTY ANGEL

I tend to think of my sister as one of a kind, a genuine original. And in the ways that count, she really is, but she has a double, who so closely resembles her, at least in physical appearance, that casual acquaintances cannot easily tell them apart. The way we learned of this girl's existence is rather amusing. Let me tell you.

One of Bootsy's favorite haunts in the Houston area is a Mexican restaurant called *Fiesta en Guadalajara*, which is quite near her art studio. Bootsy's first book-signing for *Dusky Nightshade and the Little Heathens* took place on the shaded patio of that establishment. A year later a similar event at the same location followed publication of her second book, *Baring All*. At that time she was five months pregnant. A week or two later her yet-unknown doppelganger happened to be dining at Fiesta en Guadalajara when a concerned waitress asked whether she had lost her baby. I can only imagine the conversation that ensued. In any case, it soon became clear that the young lady in question was not, in fact, the author Trudy Silverheels.

The manager on duty became interested, and locating one of Bootsy's business cards beside the cash register, she called the studio to invite Bootsy to come meet her "long-lost twin." Intrigued, Bootsy asked me to drive her to the restaurant. I just happened to be visiting there when the call came in, you see. Percy accompanied us as well.

PA Jalili is from a conservative, respectable Philippine-American family with very traditional values. She initially declined to tell us her real name, saying that she preferred to go by her initials only. We later learned that *PA* stands for *Pretty Angel.* I don't blame her for not wanting to reveal her name. What was her mother thinking?

At first, I was not terribly impressed by PA's superficial resemblance to Bootsy. True, her face had the same general shape and her brown eyes had Bootsy's very-becoming epicanthic fold, but that seemed to be all. PA's nose, mouth, and hair were slightly different, as were her complexion (her coloring, I mean), her mannerisms, and her voice. Still, I could see how a stranger might see them as similar. Then I noticed that PA's left eye occasionally exhibited that laziness that Bootsy's often did. I immediately became suspicious that the two of them might actually be related.

Bootsy's natural father, Stoney Gorman, it turns out, is well acquainted with PA's mother, who has visited his studio in Tuba City, Arizona, frequently in order to purchase silver-and-turquoise Navajo jewelry from him. Of course, PA refuses to even consider the possibility that Stoney could be her real father, but in my mind there is no doubt whatsoever. His eyes are quite like

Bootsy's and PA's, even to the detail of the left one's being reluctant to track with the right. Having never married, Stoney has no legitimate offspring. And yet he has spread his seed far and wide.

PA is five or six years Bootsy's junior. The two of them could hardly be less alike in character and personality. PA is in an exclusive relationship with one young man and works at a steady job. She is a teacher's aide in a preschool. Or at least, she was until recently. A series of arrests for possession of a controlled substance may well have wrecked that career. I cannot say with authority.

After the cave-in, when Bootsy gave up hope of appearing as herself in a proposed video production of *Baring All*, she urged PA to try out for the rôle. PA agreed and seemed eager for the opportunity to portray Bootsy on the small screen. But then of a sudden she just dropped out of sight. She no longer answers our telephone calls. Nor does she respond to our emails. Except that we see her name from time to time on the Police Blotter, we might assume that she has died.

Bootsy is prepared to embrace PA as a sister. And the rest of us are just as anxious to be her friends. But PA seems not to want to have anything more to do with us. It is a very frustrating situation. And I don't know anything more to say about it. &

XI
WORLD TRAVELER

On Bootsy's Twitter-account profile, she describes herself as a Native American author, model, artists, photographer, and world traveler. When we were children, we made frequent trips with our mother. It seemed as if we were always on the go, visiting new places. Apparently, this is what got Bootsy hooked on travel. It had the opposite effect on me. Having already seen many an exotic land, I prefer now to remain at home in familiar surroundings and let the world come to me. I'm not sure I even know all the trips Bootsy has made abroad. She mentioned four overseas journeys in *Baring All*, but she neglected to say anything whatever about the odyssey I find most fascinating.

She was living in Austin, Texas, a few years ago when the work of a certain fine-art photographer in the Ukraine came to her attention. She instantly fell in love with the images this man produced. She yearned to pose for him herself. For weeks she agonized over the fact that he was so far away. Finally, relying on translation software, she contacted him and explained her desire to work with him. He seemed to like the snapshots of her she sent him, for he wanted to hire her for three full days if she cared to make the trip. Unfortunately, the modeling fee he offered, although very generous, was not enough to cover the entire cost of the trip. Still, he suggested a few other photographers and painters in Eastern Europe that might also wish to engage her. She then contacted each of them, and one thing led to another. She ended up circumnavigating the globe, paying for the whole trip herself by sitting for well-known artists in twelve different countries: Ukraine, Russia, Hungary, Belarus, France, England, Spain, Italy, Indonesia, Thailand, China, and Japan. She was even able to bank a few thousand dollars when she got back home. Nor did she encounter any monumental difficulties along the way.

That girl has always had the most fantastic good luck. Of course, she would probably argue that her good luck has more to do with meticulous research, detailed planning, and careful preparation than with notoriously fickle fortune. And I suppose I'd have to concede the point. Still, I cannot but be impressed by how things always seem to turn out well for my sister. Oh, she's had her share of mishaps, but she's like that proverbial cat that always lands on its feet.

Bootsy's least favorite mode of transportation is flying. She avoids air planes when she can, preferring, instead, ships, trains, or buses. She drives, of course, but only ever locally. She has never in her adult life made a long car trip, and she swears she never will. We both got enough of automobile travel as little girls.

Earlier this year Bootsy talked me into taking a ten-day banana-boat tour of the Caribbean with her. Our mother had bought and paid for tickets for herself and Bea, but then circumstances had forced her to cancel their trip, and the tickets were not refundable at the last minute.

I've been on cruise ships before, but let me tell you, a working banana boat is a whole different matter. The accommodations are less luxurious, to be sure, but the total experience is one of elegance. We even dressed for dinner every night. There being only six passenger cabins, we got to know our fellow travelers rather well. It was like being in an Agatha Christi novel, but happily, without the murder. Daytime amusements included shuffleboard on deck, skeet shooting out over the water, sunbathing, and reading. There was no swimming, except when we stopped at some island with a beach. Evening activities included contract bridge, other card games and board games, dancing, karaoke, and drinking. Neither Bootsy nor I ever imbibe in alcohol, but a goodly number of our fellow travelers did.

From time to time one of the passengers would organize a party, and we'd all play naughty charades, truth-or-dare, strip poker, or some other game meant to take us out of our comfort zones and thrust us into unaccustomed familiarity with people we barely knew. Occasionally these goings-on went a little too far, and yet not far enough to put anyone at risk for contracting an STD.

Things always stopped short of fucking or sucking, but not always before a bit of grab-ass.

At first, being a respectable married lady, I was timid about allowing myself to be drawn into these rather questionable shenanigans, but Bootsy easily persuaded me to let myself go. I'm glad she made the effort. I enjoyed myself immensely as soon as I quit worrying what Geoffrey's parents might think. As for Geoffrey himself, I knew he'd be okay with it. We have an understanding.

On another occasion Bootsy flew to the Cayman Islands for an underwater nude photo shoot, her first underwater shoot and apparently the photographer's first as well. Of more than a hundred exposures, fewer than half a dozen shots were usable. Oh, they were in sharp focus alright, the lighting was good, and the composition (always a bit of a challenge underwater) was quite acceptable. The problem was a matter of simple physics: namely that adipose tissue is lighter than water. Had Bootsy and her photographer considered this basic fact, she would not have been posed in the upright position in most of the pictures. Instead, she would have been diving downward or swimming horizontally across the screen. Unfortunately, in almost every shot, her feet were down and her head was up. In that attitude her breasts floated upward, as if trying desperately to reach her face. The result looked too absurd. Most of what was shot that day could never be shown and had to be permanently deleted. The photographer was as determined as was Bootsy that no one else ever see those images. Bootsy happily agreed to do a re-shoot for free.

Modeling for cosplay conventions afforded Bootsy a great opportunity for domestic travel. Dressed up as a popular manga character and in a group of five or six other girls, she would prance out onto a small stage, slashing about with a samurai sword or making threatening gestures with a firearm heavier than she could possibly have discharged with any accuracy. But anime fans ate it up. Bootsy never make a whole lot of money doing this type of modeling, but she had fun, and she got to visit San Antonio, Los Angeles, San Diego, Seattle, St Louis, Chicago, and Atlanta. This was whilst she was in graduate school at UT in Austin.

හ

XII
SEX FRIENDS

My sister religiously practices safer sex. She has numerous lovers, both male and female—*sex friends*, she calls them—but with only one (Percy Cabot, the father of her twins) has she ever enjoyed unprotected sex. That pretty much means no oral sex with anyone else. Lots of people believe that oral sex is not dangerous, but Bootsy thinks differently. "Any pink-on-pink contact," she insists, "poses more of a risk than I care to face." I've heard her say those words a hundred times.

To be perfectly honest, she has occasionally given blow jobs, but only with flavored condoms. And that's not a very satisfying way to get your cock sucked, or so I'm told. Bootsy has also been on the giving and the receiving end of cunnilingus a few times (very few), but only with the protection of dental dam (a little latex sheet laid over the vulva). And again that's not very satisfying for the one licking, because the only taste she experiences is of latex and whatever it is flavored with.

And yet there are lots of other ways for lovers to give each other pleasure, and Bootsy has mastered them all. She tells me that she always finds her sexual encounters exquisitely enjoyable, and she makes absolutely certain that her lovers have equally rewarding experiences. She claims never to have been disappointed sexually by anyone, for she is fully committed to bringing out the best in every partner. What makes this work, I think, is a positive and optimistic attitude, undemanding flexibility, genuine affection for all her paramours, and boundless generosity. No one could possibly be a great lover without these qualities.

In a way, *sex friends* is a really accurate way to describe Bootsy's lovers —the men anyway—for each was a good friend before being invited to become her paramour as well. And long after her sex appeal has faded, she and her former lovers will still be close friends. I am confident of that. Nor do all Bootsy's male friends receive that coveted invitation to become her sex friend. As cute and winsome and desirable as my sister is, just about anyone who knows her is in love with her. And while she values all her friends, she simply cannot allow them all to become her lovers.

"There's only so much of me to go around," she explains. "If I spread myself too thin, I'd never find time to write, to do art and photography, or to play with the twins."

So it is an elite brotherhood, the male sex friends of Bootsy Silverheels. Half the members are over fifty years of age, and all are men of accomplishment: creative geniuses every one of them. When you understand Bootsy, as I believe I do, that will not seem strange or surprising. In truth, Bootsy is not sexually attracted to men at all. She'll flip for any pretty girl. But the only men able to excite Bootsy's libido are those she so admires and looks up to that she wants to be them (or at the very least, to be just like them). Coitus is her way of merging with them. When she has sex with a man, she is attempting to become him. Anyway, that's my theory.

Her sexual encounters with other girls are an entirely different matter. If she finds some cute young thing attractive and willing, she doesn't even have to know the girl's name. She's ready to hop into bed with her. Of course, that doesn't mean that none of Bootsy's female sex friends are as close to her heart as the men she loves. A few definitely are (Cricket Firestone, Bambi Nguyen, Dana Mars, and perhaps some other I haven't met yet).

The late Christopher Hitchens (author of *God Is not Great*, *The Portable Atheist*, *Arguably*, *Mortality*, and goodness knows how many other books) was a close friend of Bootsy's, and I always assumed that they were lovers. Not so, she tells me. She invited him once to become her sex friend, but he declined "with sincere regrets." Having cheated on his first wife, he was absolutely determined never to commit such an egregious offense again. His relationship with Carol Blue was far too precious to risk destroying.

In *Baring All*, Bootsy claimed to have been on intimate terms with "no fewer than seventeen penises." Before starting that particular chapter, she actually made a list of all the men with whom she had been sexually intimate. Sitting at my breakfast table one morning, sipping coffee, she scribbled their names (or in one case a descriptive identifier) on a paper napkin. I still have it; though it's no longer a complete list. Here follows that list as written:

Sammy Martinez

Claudio Beltrán

Mr Hamasaki

Dewey Applequist

Ross Lamar Berenson

Ian Shaw

Damien Wynter

Percy Cabot

Simon Estes

Randy Nakamura

Leo Madrigal

Casper Nash

Sebastian Drake

Ed Hardesty

Avery Baqa
A Spanish youth in Barcelona
Donald Freund

I thought about adding a brief explanation of who each of these individuals is or was and how Bootsy happened to know him, but I think I shall leave that to my sister. She has already mentioned most of these men in her own writing, and probably she intends to write about the others at a later time.

Bootsy and I represent the third generation of sexually liberated women in our family. Mother and Gran were both quite promiscuous as young girls. So it is hardly surprising that my sister and I should be as adventurous and uninhibited as they. I think we were born knowing about the birds and the bees. I cannot remember a time when sex was mysterious to either my sister or me; nor a time when it was not urgently important to us. I was twelve before I managed to get laid. But I was already expert at blow jobs and hand jobs. I enjoyed the reputation of a girl that liked to make out, especially with older boys. Bootsy was not quite eleven the first time she went all the way. And she was far from inexperienced then.

Mind you, our mother and grand-mother were unaware of our early sex lives. But had they known, I wonder whether they would have objected overmuch. It would have been pretty hypocritical of them if they had. No, I believe they have the same attitude that Bootsy and I have: that sex is always and necessarily a good thing, wholesome, natural, and spiritually rewarding. ∽

XIII
COLLECTING

Bootsy has been a collector of beautiful objects since she was a little girl. Our cousin Michelle gave her a medicine bag in 1993. It contained a single obsidian arrowhead. To that medicine bag Bootsy has added other items over the years: an Indian-head coin, some smooth stones, seashells, an antique thimble, a pair of curious old buttons, and a small gold nugget. This traditional Native American talisman she wears around her neck. But her penchant for collecting goes way beyond found objects to place inside her medicine bag.

Before we moved to Mexico City in 1998, Mother worked in an art gallery in Albuquerque, New Mexico; so Bootsy had plenty of opportunity to be acquainted with the lovely creations displayed there. She also visited other art galleries quite alone and began her own collection of fine art at age eight with the purchase of a small aquatint etching by Percy Cabot, whom she would someday meet and fall in love with.

Today her collection fills Primrose Cottage to overflowing and transforms that unpretentious little house into a quite-extraordinary art museum. Bootsy owns works by Karen Noles and Karen Roberts, Steve Hanks, Leo Madrigal, Flor Garduño, Antonio Macedo, Marcus J Ranum, Olivia, Nobuyoshi Araki, Patrick Nagel, Mario Tauzin, Monique Weston, Sydney Long, Randy Nakamura, Zhao Kailin, Jack Vettriano, and others Incidentally, she has posed for a number of the painters, sculptors, and photographers whose works are in her collection. Her favorite theme, of course, is erotica. But she also has a few landscapes, a still life or two, several portraits, and even some non-objective abstracts.

Bootsy collects posters and reproductions as well, but these less-valuable items are kept in Houston at her studio in the Griffoun Society's new temporary clubhouse. She buys and reads countless books every year, but she retains very few of these, preferring, instead, to donate them to the Griffoun Society library. Her music collection, the greatest concentration of which is in salsa, samba, jazz, swing, and blues, is maintained in three Sony CD changers hooked up together, each machine holding up to four hundred CDs. Bootsy is simply incapable of doing anything by halves.

Not surprisingly, her innocent little collection of sex toys has now become a major obsession with her. She seems determined to acquire an example of every device ever invented for the purpose of erotic stimulation. The focus, of course, is on aids for women, but she also owns and occasionally uses on gentlemen of her acquaintance Fleshlights and gel masturbators. She shuns only whips and anything else that delivers pain or causes humiliation.

On video once we watched Howard Stern persuade Carmen Electra to try out a device called a *Sybian*.

"I have to have one of those," Bootsy asserted.

And when she added it to her wish list on Amazon, some online acquaintances of hers suggested that she might wish also to consider another machine called a *Monkey Rocker*. So she looked it up and added it as well. I don't believe she has acquired either of these high-end toys yet. But if she ever does, I mean to make use of it as well. I assume she would be planning to keep it in one of my guest rooms, for these devices are quite large and take up more space than Bootsy has to spare in her little house.

⁊ɔ

XIV
PORNOGRAPHY AND AMBITION

Bootsy has always steadfastly refused to pose for pornography. Mind you, she does not in any way disapprove of porn. In fact, she's very fond of it. She is a particular fan of Tanner Mayes and Capri Anderson; and just this week she added to her list of favorites two Eastern European girls known only by their first names: Katka and Caprice.

According to my sister, one of the very best websites for high-class porn, or as she prefers to call it, *explicit erotica*, is X-Art. She visits often. I think that's where she first discovered Katka. Recently she was surprised to recognize in an X-Art video a couple of old friends from San Ángel. Appearing under a false name, Mindy Applequist was getting her ass drilled by her husband Dewey. So exquisitely erotic was this video, Bootsy decided that she had to give anal sex a try herself. She did not, incidentally, care for the experience and refuses ever to do it again.

When Bootsy mentioned to Mindy having seen her in a porn video, Mindy told Bootsy that the video and some still shots had earned her and Dewey ten thousand dollars, plus a trip to Florida, where the four-day shoot took place. Bootsy should give it a go, Mindy recommended. Unlike most other porn producers, X-Art allows a girl to supply her own partner if she prefers not to be paired with their Mr X. She can even go solo or with another girl.

Not having to do sex with a stranger satisfies one of Bootsy's objections to appearing in pornography, but not the other. Bootsy aspires to some yet-unspecified public-service job later in life. She hates politics, and so it is doubtful she would ever run for elected office. But as a celebrated author, bilingual and well educated, she might hope, in the distant future, depending on what else she does between now and then, to be appointed to a position of some responsibility, perhaps even ambassador to a small Third World country.

Of course, her dream job would be Librarian of Congress. Since 1800 there have been only thirteen Librarians of Congress. So she's not very hopeful about that. But one never knows what's in store, and that's why Bootsy is careful never to do anything that might come to light at an inauspicious moment and wreck her chances of confirmation. ∞

XV
BAMBI AND CARLITA

One of the girls with whom Bootsy lived in the Griffoun Dormitory is Bambi Nguyen, who happens now to live in Kemah, just outside Houston. When Bootsy decided to establish her art studio in Houston, she made a point to look up Bambi, and they renewed their friendship. That was in 2010.

About that time, my husband and I decided to purchase a house in the Houston area. We needed a second home. Geoffrey, an engineering executive for an oil company, is required to spend lots of time in Houston. He could, of course, simply stay in a hotel whenever his job takes him there, but sometimes, if we know it's going to be a long stay, the girls and I like to accompany him. And anyway, real estate is almost always a safe long-term investment.

As it happens, Bambi's mother is a real-estate agent in Pasadena, one of the communities we were most interested in looking at. Bootsy arranged for us (Bootsy and me) to meet Bambi's mother at her office. Bambi herself, being off work for reasons I don't recall and having nothing else in particular planned for the day, decided to join us as well. Ms. Nguyen's two-door Honda could have accommodated all four of us, but not so comfortably as my four-door Jaguar. So, when we set out to look at houses, I drove. Ms. Nguyen was in the front seat with me; Bootsy and Bambi were in the back seat together.

It was raining that day, as it had been raining for a week. If we were to wait for a sunny day, we might be waiting longer than I wanted to be away from home. I was eager to find a house I could love and return to Mexico City, so Geoffrey could then come, look it over, and make the final decision. We walked through houses in Pasadena, Kemah, Baytown, Texas City, and Clear Lake. The rain fell harder and harder. At times, as we drove from one location to another, I was forced (by being unable to see beyond the hood ornament) to stop the car at the side of the road until the downpour let up.

I was never aware of doing anything dangerous. I ignored no posted warning signs. And yet, somehow we got caught up in a flash flood. The car stalled, and I attempted to restart it, but the water was rising rapidly, and the next thing we knew we were being swept away in a furious current. It was a terrifying ordeal, but we all survived. When the car became lodged in a little coppice of live oak trees, we exited through the windows. Then holding hands, we four slogged through waist-deep water to solid ground. I almost said *dry ground*. But there was no dry ground for a hundred miles around.

My Jaguar, not yet a month old, was a total loss. I told Geoffrey on the phone and asked him what I should do about it.

"Just let our insurance company know. Then go pick out a new one. I'll make sure your account has enough to cover the check."

It is a blessing to be wealthy. Money doesn't solve all problems, but it certainly works magic on most. I am fully cognizant that I have never done anything to deserve such good fortune. The simple truth is that I married well. Nor was I even aware at the time that my intended was well on his way to being rich. At age seventeen, all I knew about Geoffrey was that I could not imagine my life without him. We fell in love at first sight, and he has never let me down in any way.

Now, that doesn't mean he doesn't stray from time to time. But that's only to be expected. I am not so unreasonable as to demand that he never take an interest in other women. As long as I have his loyalty and his love, I am content. I understand that he is going to philander a bit. All men do, or else they wish they had the nerve to. It is in their nature.

In any event, I found the perfect house in Clear Lake (five bedrooms, three and a half baths, attached garage, and unlike our house in Mexico City, ultra modern). We closed on it in record time. Then we bought two new vehicles to keep in the garage (exact duplicates of the two vehicles we drove in Mexico City, a Jaguar and a Land Rover). Thus we should have familiar transportation whenever we flew into town for the weekend or to stay for a few months.

In order that the house not remain empty whilst we were away, I asked Bootsy if she'd house-sit for us. It would relieve her of the need to pay rent on an apartment. She was not expected to stay at home every night, for I knew that she liked to sleep with Percy a couple of nights a week. And naturally, she had trysts with other lovers as well, but usually those were not all-nighters. I also asked Bootsy to make a point of driving each of the vehicles regularly. Cars don't do well when they just sit idle for weeks at a time, or so Geoffrey tells me.

Bootsy let go her apartment and rented a small studio in the same building. The old apartment had boasted a queen-size bed; the new studio had no bed at all, but it was half the price. And that is the way things stood until Carlita came into our lives.

A young Apache woman from Chihuahua, Carlita Her-Name-Means-Thunder Wakiya, is a Mexican national. She speaks English, but not well. Her Spanish is only a little better. The ancient Apache tongue is her cradle language. She was a housewife when Bootsy first met her. She and her husband lived in a rental house only a few blocks from the studio. Almost daily Bootsy and Carlita ran into each other at the neighborhood bakery and inevitably became pals. Both of them being Native American, they had an automatic connection.

Carlita seems to be a certifiable nymphomaniac. Had her husband Manuel been able to spend every minute of every day with her, she would have been perfectly content with him. She would have had no need of other men. But left alone for eight or ten hours a day whilst he worked, she went crazy. She needed company—human contact—all the time, constantly. And the only way she had ever known how to relate to men was sexually. She didn't relate well to other women at all. Bootsy was her first girlfriend, maybe because Bootsy didn't seem to disapprove of her as other women in the neighborhood did.

The fact that Bootsy and Carlita both have multiple lovers might, to the casual observer, make them seem alike in character. But the truth is that they are extreme opposites. In the first place, Bootsy is honest about her relationships. She has never cheated, because she has never sworn to be faithful to anyone. Then too, every single one of Bootsy relationships are precious to her. She loves and respects all her sex friends. Carlita has casual sex with anyone, even total strangers. She takes terrible chances with her life and her safety. Over and over again she has set herself up for humiliation. Bootsy would never do that. But the biggest difference is that Bootsy's lifestyle is a conscious choice and it makes Bootsy happy. Carlita's outrageous behavior is involuntary and pathological. It only causes her misery. She would change if she could.

In Northside Village Carlita's exploits were well known, except to her husband, who thought she was a perfect angel, until the day he came home from work early and found her in bed with his brother. Sounds like a cliché, I know, but it's the absolute gospel truth, I swear. Manuel very nearly beat her to death. Then he and his brother fled the country together back to their native Mexico before he could be arrested. I suppose Manuel found it easy to forgive his brother, Carlita being so irresistible.

Bootsy visited Carlita in hospital, and when Carlita was eventually released, Bootsy invited her to stay at the studio. It was a work space only, but there was a small sofa upon which she could sleep. It might not be very comfortable, but it would beat sleeping in the park. Percy's apartment was just down the hall. She could use his bathroom, keep house and cook for him. Percy wasn't keen on this arrangement, but he went along (and graciously too). If Bootsy willed it, he was on board one hundred per cent.

I love to see that kind of loyalty. Indeed, I value loyalty above any other quality in a friend or lover. I cannot say too much about it.

But now, back to Carlita. She was in a bad position, She had been totally dependent on her husband, and now she was alone and adrift. She had no money. She had no job. She had no skills (other than domestic), and she showed little interest in acquiring new skills. In the country illegally, she didn't even have an ID or a Social Security card. There was never any doubt that she would accept Bootsy's generous offer of shelter.

"She thinks you don't like her, darling," said Bootsy to Percy at the end of Carlita's first week there.

"I declined her invitation to have sex with her. That's all."

"But why? Don't you find her attractive? I'm not possessive or jealous, you know."

"I do know. But it just doesn't feel right. She's pretty enough—not beautiful, by any means—but sexually alluring nonetheless. Still, I don't have any affection for her. That might not have mattered when I was younger, but somehow it does now. I can't explain."

Nevertheless, Percy remained willing to have Carlita stay at the studio. He seemed not to consider her presence an imposition at all. She was a splendid housekeeper. But her cooking was uninspired. She only knew how to prepare a very few dishes. Those she did well, but Percy wanted more variety. So he began teaching her how to prepare other foods than just Mexican rice, pinto beans, *caldo*, *fajitas*, *tortillas*, and rice pudding. She really seemed to enjoy learning these new recipes. Percy was surprised, because she had been so terribly uninterested in learning studio skills that would have been a real help to him and Bootsy and might have allowed Carlita to earn enough of an income to make her independent.

When Bootsy established Silverheels Trading Post online and Percy opened an identically named retail outlet in a shopping mall, Bootsy realized pretty quickly that she needed to start spending more time at the studio, building pencil boxes, birdhouses, chests, furniture, dream-catchers, jewelry, and other items to sale. She asked me to consider allowing Carlita to move into the house in Clear Lake in order that she (Bootsy) might be able to move back into her own art studio. She did warn me that Carlita was almost certain to try to seduce Geoffrey.

"I trust him to always use a condom. But can I trust Carlita not to rob us blind or throw wild parties?"

"I believe so. I trust her. She doesn't drive though. I'll still have to take your cars out for a spin every now and then, and that will give me an excuse to look in on her."

So I agreed, and Bootsy and Carlita changed places. Bootsy's studio was very tiny, almost too cramped to be an effective work space. An old camper trailer in the back yard was then converted to a picture-frame shop, and Bootsy was able to move all the woodworking tools out of the studio and into this trailer. In fact, she pulled everything out and started over, decorating the studio to be a living space. It turned out beautifully.

Carlita is still with us, minding the house whilst we are away. Her English is improving. And she takes on odd jobs around the neighborhood to earn extra income for herself. She told me once that Bootsy and Percy had been such an inspiration to her that she meant to try to become more like them. I think she really meant it, but I wonder whether, on her own, without the help of a psychotherapist, she really can change. ∽

XVI
PROSTITUTION

It is a firm policy with Bootsy never to write about anything of which she has no knowledge. Not being a historian, she never sets her tales in ages past or in places she has not herself lived, or at the very least, visited. Any description she writes can be counted upon to be absolutely accurate in every detail. Therefore, when she decided to tell the story of a teenage prostitute, she knew that she had a lot of research to do before she could even begin typing.

The videographer Napoleon Plum and his partner Dana Mars (a former dorm mate of Bootsy's at the Griffoun Society in Austin) have studios in both Austin and Mérida, Yucatan, Mexico. Napoleon is known to call on prostitutes with some regularity. He was able to give Bootsy some basic information, such as typical prices for various services and a fact or two that did not exactly square with the strong and appealing character she wished to create.

"In the first place," said Napoleon, "most, if not all, street whores are addicts. They have no particular skills and no professional pride. If they can figure out a way to get your money without doing anything for you, scruples will never get in their way. Is this the kind of girl you intend to write about?'

"No," Bootsy confessed. "My heroine is going to be the exact opposite of the girls you describe. But I shan't present her as typical. She must be extraordinary in every way. But I still need to know everything she would have to know in order to survive on the street."

"Do you want me to introduce you to one of my favorites?"

"Absolutely. Is she an addict?"

"Of course. If you want to meet a prostitute who is not an addict, you'll have to visit a bordello. Maybe I can arrange that. I'll see what I can do."

"But aren't there any high-class call girls, like in the movies?"

"Oh, sure, in large cities. But they are way out of my price range. And I wouldn't begin to know how to locate one."

"Tell me this, Napoleon, if you can. Why do men go to prostitutes anyway?"

Napoleon chuckled. "I should have thought that was pretty obvious."

"Come on. I'm not stupid. I know it's for sex. And if a guy is so unattractive that he doesn't have much chance of getting laid otherwise, it makes sense. But why do men with loving wives or steady girlfriends patronize hookers?"

"Two reasons, I guess: variety and sexual independence."

Bootsy asked him to elaborate.

"I never like to do the same girl twice in a row. If someone is really good, I'll definitely want to come back to her, but not immediately. I always prefer that my next sexual encounter be with someone other than the last girl I had. That's what keeps it exciting."

"And what about *sexual indepen-dence*?"

"I refuse to be dependent on someone else's whim or mood for my sexual gratification. If I feel like having sex, I hate to be denied or put off. I know I sound spoiled. But on the other hand I cannot think of any good reason why I shouldn't have what I want when I want it. I accept that wives and girl-friends cannot be expected always to be ready to cater to a man's pleasure. Sometimes they really do have headaches. But as long as there are prostitutes, I never have to do without, and I never have to wait. Do you blame me?"

"No. If I were a man, I'm pretty certain that your attitude would be mine as well."

That evening Napoleon drove Boot-sy to Sixth Street in downtown Austin to meet an eighteen-year-old hooker called *Destiny*, who allowed Bootsy to accompa-ny her to work. Destiny's real name was *Sherlyn*, and Bootsy was mildly surprised at how much she liked the girl.

Sherlyn introduced Bootsy to her first client of the night as her parole officer. "She needs to see how I earn my living. You don't mind if she watches, do you?"

To another client, Sherlyn said she was showing Bootsy the ropes. "She'll be on the job next week. You'll have to come back and look her up."

"What's your name, honey?" the man asked Bootsy.

"*Danger.* Just call me *Danger.*"

"Start tonight, Danger. I'll pay triple for a doubleheader."

"Sorry. I don't have my union card yet."

The man had a good sense of humor. He laughed appreciatively, then paid Sherlyn a hundred dollars for a quick fuck in the back seat of his Cadillac.

Three weeks later Napoleon invited Bootsy to meet him in Mérida, where he introduced her to a "consummate professional," a girl named *Karen*, who, at age twenty-four, already owned her own *casa de citas* (house of assignations). As Bootsy looked on, Karen did Napoleon herself.

"I only do this for special customers," she explained afterward. "I have six other girls, and they do all the walk-ins."

When Napoleon said goodbye, Bootsy stayed behind to interview her new acquaintance further. Karen was amazingly candid, extremely intelligent, delightfully personable, and ruthlessly ambitious.

"Do you want to take the next customer?"

"I don't think so. Thanks for offering though."

"If you really want to know about my profession, you need to practice it. At least once."

"I was almost persuaded," Bootsy confided to me later. "But then she showed me the CCTV monitors in her office. She meant to reassure me that I'd be safe, because she's be watching. But I figured that if there were cameras, there probably was recording equipment as well. I don't want a video like that ever coming back to haunt me."

Not long after that, we read that Karen had been arrested in a massive sting operation. She was facing charges not only of prostitution (a misdemeanor), but also of organized criminal activity (a felony). She was in a world of trouble. Of course, she had a battery of high-powered attorneys to defend her. Bootsy, while wishing Karen good luck, felt extremely fortunate not to have been in the house herself when it was raided.

We were having lunch together at a sidewalk café in the Zona Rosa as she was telling me about her adventures in the demimonde.

"Would you really have serviced a client if you hadn't found out about the cameras?" I asked.

"Yeah, I think so. It was right on the tip of my tongue to say okay."

"And whatever happened to your determination never to allow penetration by anyone unworthy of you?"

Bootsy shrugged. "I still feel that way. If I didn't, it would have been a much easier decision. But there are other factors to be weighed. First, I now consider the experience of doing sex for money as vital research. And second, my customer, with any luck, would never know my true identity."

I laughed. "You'd be like the Catholic girl in the gymnasium shower who covers only her face when strange men wander through."

"I read that book too," she told me. "Isn't it funny how everything you read becomes a part of you?"

Now, as it happened, there were, at another much-larger table in the same outdoor restaurant, a group of six American teenage boys. Giddy with the excitement of being in a foreign land, out from under the thumbs of their too-strict families (probably for the first time ever), and believing that no one within earshot could understand English, they were talking rather too loudly, discussing how best to go about connecting with local prostitutes. What a fortuitous coincidence!

"Silly nerds!" Bootsy whispered.

"They're the opportunity you've been waiting for. If you don't help 'em out, they'll never get laid. They're as clueless as Old Jupiter."

That made her smile. "I'll do it if you will."

"It's a deal," I said without giving myself any opportunity to weigh the matter properly.

We paid our cheque and lingered over coffee till we saw the young men get up to leave. Then we followed them out, and on the sidewalk we insinuated ourselves into their group.

"I hope you boys have plenty of American dollars," Bootsy said in English, but with a fake Mexican accent, "because what you're looking for don't come cheap."

We started out by asking three hundred dollars from each of them. That was way more than they had. So we haggled and eventually agreed to do it for "a third of our regular price."

"But only because you're such cute boys," Bootsy added. "We like American boys a lot. I hope you got some whatcha-call-ems: c*ondominiums.*"

It was an old joke, but she made it seem like an honest mistake, which they found absolutely delightful. I asked if they were all at least eighteen, and they swore solemnly that they were. Still, I meant to see proof, but with everyone talking at once I never got around to asking for IDs before the party got underway.

It wouldn't do for us to be seen entering their hotel with them; so we sent them ahead, and five minutes later we entered the lobby and went straight to the elevators. When we knocked on the door to their suite, they let us in and promptly handed over our combined fee, six hundred dollars. I am confident that they would tell you they got good value for their money.

On the ride down in the elevator, Bootsy leaned close to my ear and whispered, "Whore!"

I had to laugh. I wanted terribly to make a clever retort, but all I could think to reply was, "Takes one to know one."

A few months later Bootsy's novella, *The Chosen Profession of Jade Stonecalf*, saw print. ❧

XVII
LITTLE WARRIOR GIRL

One spring day, when Bootsy was not yet three years old, she tied a bath towel around her neck to make herself a cape, then ran through the house, belting out her off-key version of a heroic Wagnerian theme, her terry-cloth cape flying behind her. Repeatedly, she climbed up onto the arm of an over-stuffed chair and leapt off. This Gran tolerated only because Bootsy looked so cute doing it. Usually feet on the furniture were strictly forbidden, and unnecessary noise was always frowned upon. Predictably, Gran's tolerance soon began to wear thin.

"Alright, Superman, take it outside."

Indignant, Bootsy informed Gran that she was not Superman.

"Well then, Batgirl, or whoever you are—"

Clearly offended that her true identity had not been immediately appreciated, Bootsy cut Gran off in mid-sentence. Glowering ominously, she intoned, "I'm God."

And that was the end of that. Nobody argues with God or tells her to go out of doors.

My sister has always had a way of taking charge of every situation. She refuses to allow the world, life in general, or ill fortune to get the best of her for very long. Nor has she ever permitted others to define who she is. She is truly writing her own story. Kismet has not a chance with Bootsy. As for Karma, well, Karma loves her.

I don't think Mother Theresa was any more committed to doing good in the world than is my sister. Bootsy has simply elected to follow a different strategy as a champion of enlightenment. Her war name, by the way, is *Baa' Yázhí*, which, in the Navajo tongue, means *Little Warrior Girl*. She is prepared at a moment's notice to do battle for any just cause. And yet she prefers never to contend against any of her fellow human beings. The enemies she attacks, showing no mercy, are ignorance, hatred, greed, prejudice, superstition, and intolerance. Imagine the struggle as that of a raiding party. She leads by example.

Like all the great sages throughout the millennia, Bootsy loves everyone within the human family, and even more remarkably, she finds something to like about most people. She told me recently, and in all sincerity, I believe, that she wishes there were a way to be personally acquainted with every human being alive in the world today. She values people and finds no one uninteresting. The very fact that we are all different makes each person uniquely fascinating to her. And just about anyone who has the opportunity to know Bootsy is the richer for it.

She maintains a presence on MySpace, Facebook, LinkedIn, and other social-media sites. She confirms all friend requests and tries to answer all friendly messages. She enjoys online chats, but really doesn't have time to engage with everyone who wants to chat with her. It would be a physical impossibility. Those who accept this reality and are content to correspond by email or on-site messaging will find the relationship rewarding.

And what a splendid sense of humor has my little sister! A day never passes that she doesn't make me laugh. When she was pregnant and her back ached all the time, I commiserated with her and reminded her that I had been in her shoes.

"I knew it," she snapped back. "You gave me athlete's foot."

Her Tweets are sometimes funny; sometimes helpful or insightful; but always clever. Occasionally she even uses her Twitter account to recommend or pan a motion picture. A few examples of Bootsy's Tweets that I thought interesting enough to save are included as an appendix to this work

Incidentally, Bootsy also writes and posts book reviews and movie reviews on various internet sites, including Amazon and Good Reads.

She has an interesting philosophy regarding literature and drama. She believes that any work worthy of being called *art* must somehow enrich the life of the reader or viewer. There has to be a take-away, a gift, an opportunity for personal growth; or else the work in question were better never to have been created. Mind you, she is not suggesting that every worthwhile book or movie must have an obvious moral. That kind of heavy-handedness amounts to mere propaganda, which no one enjoys very much. But a book or a movie that tries too hard only to be entertaining without offering the reader or viewer any spiritual benefit is almost certainly going to do harm, possibly by reinforcing prejudices, by seeming to legitimize violence, or by glamorizing unhealthy lifestyle choices, such as substance abuse.   so

APPENDIX
Bootsy's Tweets

All sweeping generalities will eventually prove false, including this one.

What's so great about being normal? "Normal" just means "average."

Artificial insemination? No way! If I want your sperm, the least I can do is show my appreciation with a little nooky.

I paid extra for popcorn labeled "lite." Turns out the way they make it lite is to give you half the regular portion.

Call me crazy, but I'd almost always prefer to be screwed by a human being than by a corporation.

Never once have I seen any one's religious beliefs make him/her a better person.

I'm appalled at how few people (even TV presenters, journalists, and novelists) seem to know the difference between "I" and "me."

I've been so naughty this year, I'm bound to clean up at Christmas.

The Mafia must get a huge hoot out of jerking the FBI around by dropping hints every few years as to where Hoffa's body is buried.

Sure, I talk to myself. It's the only intelligent conversation I get anymore.

I watched <u>The Hunger Games</u> tonight. What a silly pointless movie!

Graffiti isn't art; it's vandalism.

There's a downside to sleeping nude. Mosquitoes seem to prefer those sensitive places most awkward to scratch.

The terms by which a problem is defined limit the range of possible solutions to be considered.

Who made the rule that every worthwhile endeavor must be met with stubborn, irrational resistance and seemingly insurmountable obstacles?

Rosario Dawson says penises are getting smaller. Don't be alarmed. She's talking about otters.
I used to be 100% sure about everything. Now I find it difficult to be even 90% sure about anything.

Lots of talk about compromise in Washington these days, but most politicians seem to define the word as "the other side's caving in."

Finally got to watch <u>Kama Sutra</u> with Indira Varma. What a movie masterpiece! I give it my highest recommendation.

The word "epicenter" has suddenly become very popular. And it's almost always used incorrectly, except when discussing earthquakes.

Saw <u>The Girl with the Dragon Tattoo</u>. Big surprise: I loved it. The title character is awesome.

If Necessity is the mother of Invention, then who is the mother of Re-invention?

Conservatism (political, religious, social) inevitably obstructs progress, for by its very nature it opposes change.

Conservatism always looks to the past for a model for the future.
Today someone called me a "possibilitarian." Now, that's a label I'm proud to embrace.

If you can't make friends, then whom?

People always matter more than principles, ideas, beliefs, values, governments, or churches.

Let me never demand respect, but instead simply strive to be worthy of respect.

Why do so many people want to do God's work. Isn't He big enough to take care of Himself?

It costs me nothing to be nice (even when others are not), and I feel better for it.

What's so objectionable about being thought of as a sex object? I dread the day nobody finds me exciting or alluring.

Watched <u>Friends with Benefits</u> tonight. Very disappointing! I expected better.

Anecdotal evidence of anything is evidence of nothing.

Of all my relations, I like sex best.

Suggested Reading

If you enjoyed this biographical sketch of Trudy Lynn (Bootsy) Silverheels by her sister Miranda (Dusty) Whitecrow, then you might also like these other books:

Dusky Nightshade and the Little Heathens, an illustrated novel by Trudy Silverheels

Baring All, the autobiography of Trudy Silverheels

The Chosen Profession of Jade Stonecalf, an illustrated novella by Trudy Silverheels

Nuevo Biloxi, a novel by Trudy Silverheels and Damien Wynter

Good Medicine, a commonplace book (a collection of wise sayings) originally compiled by Miranda Whitecrow, revised and updated by her sister Trudy Silverheels

Of Fairies and Witches and Kisses and Wishes, juvenile light verse by Phoebe Synn with contributions by Trudy Silverheels and others

The Adventures of Pinky Valentine and Friends, a jevenile novella by Phoebe Synn and Trudy Silverheels

Coming Clean, the collected short works (memoirs, poems, essays) of Trudy Silverheels with illustrations by the author

Daybook of a Warrior Girl, being selected entries from the diaries of Trudy Silverheels, edited by Xiomara Roma, illustrated in full color

The Trudy Silverheels Scrapbook, a picture book edited by Xiomara Roma

Model's Handbook by Percy Cabot and Trudy Silverheels, a fully illustrated guide to success in the modeling profession

www.ingramcontent.com/pod-product-compliance
Lightning Source LLC
Chambersburg PA
CBHW071756090426
42737CB00012B/1840